Today's Debates

POVERTY

Public Crisis or Private Struggle?

Joan Axelrod-Contrada
and Erin L. McCoy

Cavendish Square
New York

Published in 2019 by Cavendish Square Publishing, LLC
243 5th Avenue, Suite 136, New York, NY 10016

Copyright © 2019 by Cavendish Square Publishing, LLC

First Edition

No part of this publication may be reproduced, stored in a retrieval system, or transmitted in any form or by any means—electronic, mechanical, photocopying, recording, or otherwise—without the prior permission of the copyright owner. Request for permission should be addressed to Permissions, Cavendish Square Publishing, 243 5th Avenue, Suite 136, New York, NY 10016. Tel (877) 980-4450; fax (877) 980-4454.

Website: cavendishsq.com

This publication represents the opinions and views of the author based on his or her personal experience, knowledge, and research. The information in this book serves as a general guide only. The author and publisher have used their best efforts in preparing this book and disclaim liability rising directly or indirectly from the use and application of this book.

All websites were available and accurate when this book was sent to press.

Library of Congress Cataloging-in-Publication Data

Names: Axelrod-Contrada, Joan, author. | McCoy, Erin L., author.
Title: Poverty : needy or needing help? / Joan Axelrod-Contrada and Erin L. McCoy.
Description: New York : Cavendish Square, 2019. | Series: Today's debates |
Includes bibliographical references and index.
Identifiers: LCCN 2018019948 (print) | LCCN 2018020953 (ebook) |
ISBN 9781502643537 (ebook) | ISBN 9781502642608 (library bound) |
ISBN 9781502643520 (pbk.)
Subjects: LCSH: Poverty--United States--Juvenile literature. |
Poor--United States--Juvenile literature.
Classification: LCC HC110.P6 (ebook) | LCC HC110.P6 A923 2019 (print) |
DDC 362.50973--dc23
LC record available at https://lccn.loc.gov/2018019948

Editorial Director: David McNamara
Copy Editor: Rebecca Rohan
Associate Art Director: Alan Sliwinski
Designer: Ellina Litmanovich
Production Coordinator: Karol Szymczuk
Photo Research: J8 Media

The photographs in this book are used by permission and through the courtesy of: Cover Paul Bradbury/ OJO Images/Getty Images; p. 4 Nick Beer/Shutterstock.com; p. 10 Everett Historical/Shutterstock. com; p. 15 Fotosearch/Getty Images; p. 20 Jack Thornell/AP Images; p. 24 Rodriguez/TNS/Newscom; p. 29 Andre Chung/The Washington Post/Getty Images; p. 35 David Bacon/Alamy Stock Photo; p. 38 Mark Boster/Los Angeles Times/Getty Images; p. 43 e Ogrocki/AP Images; p. 49 Rich Pedroncelli/AP images; p. 52 Jeffrey Greenberg/UIG/Getty Images; p. 56 Bill Brett/The Boston Globe/Getty Images; p. 59 Mark Apollo/Pacific Press/Light Rocket/Getty Images; p. 62 Photographee.eu/Shutterstock. com; p. 64 Frederic J. Brown/AFP/Getty Images; p. 70 Photo/Jae C. Hong/AP Images; p. 73 Joe Raedle/Getty Images; p. 76 Chuck Kennedy/KRT/Newscom; p. 80 Matt Ryerson/The Journal-Star/ AP Images; p. 85 Aaron Huey/National Geographic/Getty Images; p. 87 Damian Dovarganes/AP Images; p. 91 Andia/ UIG/Getty Images; p. 94 Jim West/Alamy Stock Photo; p. 101 George Rose/ Getty Images; p. 103 Shawn Patrick Ouellette/Portland Press Herald/Getty Images; p. 107 Joe Appel/ Tribune-Review/AP Images; p. 109 David McNew/Getty Images; p. 112 Melissa Barnes/Aurora Photos/Alamy Stock Photo; p. 118 DGL Images/Shutterstock.com; p. 120 Al Behrman/AP Images.

Printed in the United States of America

CONTENTS

Introduction 5

Chapter One: A Brief History of Poverty in America 11

Chapter Two: How Does Poverty Happen? 25

Chapter Three: Families in Poverty 39

Chapter Four: The Suburban Poor 53

Chapter Five: The Urban Poor 65

Chapter Six: The Rural Poor 81

Chapter Seven: Homelessness and the Work Force 95

Chapter Eight: In Search of Solutions 113

Glossary 123

Further Information 124

Bibliography 127

Index 141

About the Authors 144

INTRODUCTION

Poverty can take many forms. It can mean going without basic needs—skipping meals or choosing cheaper, less-healthy foods. It can mean going without shelter or losing your job because you no longer have a car to get you to work every day. Poverty can strike suddenly, as the result of unexpected medical bills you're unable to pay or the loss of a job. And no country is immune: in the United States, one of the richest nations on earth, 40.6 million people were living in poverty in 2016, according to the US Census.

One in eight Americans, or 12.7 percent of the nation's population, lives below the official poverty line set by the US government. Many more are part of that often-overlooked group of the "near poor"—not poor

Opposite: A teenage boy in New York City in 2016 asks for spare change. He is one of millions of Americans suffering from poverty.

enough to qualify for government benefits, but too poor to live a comfortable middle-class existence. A number of complicated factors determines who experiences poverty and why, but it is first necessary to understand how poverty is defined.

Kinds of Poverty

Scholars use the terms "absolute" and "relative" to describe two kinds of deprivation associated with poverty. While absolute poverty refers to a state in which one's very survival is threatened by the lack of resources, relative poverty takes into account a person's financial situation compared to the average income and lifestyle enjoyed by the rest of the society in which he or she lives.

Economist Adam Smith offered the example of the linen shirt to illustrate the concept of relative poverty. In his 1776 book, *The Wealth of Nations*, Smith maintained that, while the linen shirt did not qualify as a necessity of life, it was an item "indecent for creditable people, even of the lowest order, to be without." Social norms varied by time and place. "The Greeks and Romans lived, I suppose, very comfortably, though they had no linen. But in the present times, through the greater part of Europe, a creditable day-laborer would be ashamed to appear in public without a linen shirt, the want of which would be supposed to denote that disgraceful degree of poverty, which, it is presumed, no body can well fall into without extreme bad conduct."

Along similar lines, few low-income Americans—the homeless are a notable exception—live in the kind of absolute poverty characteristic of the developing world. Most people in the United States enjoy amenities such as running water, electricity, and TV, which some people in Bangladesh or Kenya might consider luxuries. However, being poor in a rich land takes its own kind of toll. People with limited resources lack the power and choices of those above them on the social and economic ladder.

The Impact of Poverty

While poverty in America cuts across racial lines, it disproportionately affects minorities such as African Americans, Hispanics, and Native Americans. Those who have experienced teen pregnancy or lived in single-parent households are at higher risk of poverty. Statistics, however, tell only part of the story. Behind the numbers are real people struggling with the stress of not having enough. Something has to go. Should it be food or heat? The car or health care? Quality childcare or housing?

Invariably, one problem complicates another. The child who goes to bed hungry wakes up unable to concentrate in school, which in turn increases his or her risk of dropping out, getting low-wage work, and being unable to afford a car or decent housing. When emergencies strike, debts pile up. Without a financial cushion, many individuals and families are one step away from poverty.

Take the case of Willie Goodell. Profiled by author David K. Shipler in *The Working Poor: Invisible in America*, Willie, a roofer in his twenties, incurred $10,000 in medical bills. His teeth were decaying, but because he could not afford health insurance, he went to the emergency room rather than to a primary-care physician whenever he needed help. Because he could not pay his emergency-room bills, Willie ruined his credit rating. Meanwhile, he continued to smoke cigarettes. Sacrificing this small comfort seemed like more than he could bear.

The Debate

Who was to blame for Willie's plight? Willie himself, or society? Policymakers have long differed in their answers to such questions. While conservatives have emphasized the role of individual responsibility, liberals have pointed to the need for better economic and social support systems and safety nets. The nation's response to poverty—from poorhouses to welfare reform—has changed over time.

For generations, segregation limited the opportunities of African Americans. Even though civil rights legislation eliminated legal discrimination, inequalities remain. African Americans, for instance, are less likely than whites to inherit wealth, since they were kept in poverty as slaves for hundreds of years while whites accumulated wealth.

Increasingly, experts use the term "social capital" to describe the myriad ways in which social interactions matter. For instance, researchers have found that people from disadvantaged communities lack access to the social networks that bolster one's chances for educational and career success.

Although the United States prides itself on being a land of opportunity, the notion that anyone who is willing and able can "pull themselves up by their bootstraps" may be more myth than reality. The poor in the United States experience less economic mobility than their counterparts in other developed nations. In a report published in 2016 by the Stanford Center on Poverty and Inequality, the United States ranked sixteenth of twenty-four middle- and high-income countries with respect to intergenerational earnings mobility. In many developed countries, universal health care and greater childcare subsidies may help less advantaged members of society better reach their economic potential. Meanwhile, inside the United States, fewer children are earning more than their parents. In 2016, just 50 percent were projected to do so, compared to 90 percent in 1940. Many have attributed this change to a widening gap between the rich and the poor.

In recent years, poverty has increasingly spread into the suburbs. With the middle class besieged by stagnant wages and rising expenses, the ladder of opportunity has become more difficult to climb. In urban and rural communities, many people lead lives cut off from the American mainstream, relegated to areas of high joblessness and poor schools.

Meanwhile, workers in the United States have been hit hard by globalization and the loosening of labor regulations. Once-secure jobs in the manufacturing sector are being shipped out to low-wage workers overseas. Employees who try to organize unions to better their conditions often face an uphill battle against employers' virulent antilabor campaigns.

Can the rapidly growing service sector provide new hope for the future? If so, how can low-paying jobs, such as flipping burgers and changing bedpans, offer a living wage? What can be done to repair the holes in the safety net so that everyone has access to quality health coverage, childcare, education, and housing?

Author Robert David Rank uses the metaphor of a game of musical chairs to discuss strategies to bring more seats to America's table of plenty. Because the roots of poverty reach deep, no single solution will magically eliminate the blight. Instead, experts recommend a broad-based approach. Many argue that poverty-related problems, such as crime and poor health, cost taxpayers money that could be better spent on programs to eliminate poverty.

Saving manufacturing jobs, slowing immigration, offering universal health care, and reducing income inequality for minorities and women have all been proposed as solutions to the problem of poverty. These suggestions come from both conservative and liberal camps. However, in the game of musical chairs, collaboration may be key in finding the right combination of solutions to truly bring an end to poverty.

"'NOW THEN, GENTLEMEN, HOW MUCH DO YOU BID FOR THIS BOY?'
SAID THE AUCTIONEER."

Chapter One

A BRIEF HISTORY OF POVERTY IN AMERICA

Centuries before the United States became an independent nation, the American continents shone as beacons of opportunity and wealth for people around the globe. People came not only to flee persecution and poverty at home, but to seek out new livelihoods and more comfortable, secure futures. A look back at the history of the United States reveals shifting definitions of poverty, punctuated by periods of prosperity and economic hardship.

Seventeenth-Century Colonists

For many settlers, North America was the Land of Opportunity. Conditions in seventeenth-century England had taken a turn for the worse. The enclosure

Opposite: An indentured servant (here, fictional hero Jack Ballister) is shown being auctioned off in Virginia in 1716.

system cost many small farmers their common grazing lands, driving them into the cities to look for work. The landless poor who flocked to London in the late 1600s found a city full of drunkards, beggars, and thieves. Three out of five boys died before they reached the age of sixteen. Many people spent what little money they had on alcohol, rather than food, to dull the pain of their difficult lives.

The English government wanted to unload its convicts and surplus poor on America. Broadsides (flyers) for America portrayed the new land in glowing terms. However, few of England's poor had the money to make the trip. Nor were many enticed by the idea of journeying across the stormy Atlantic Ocean to settle in an unknown land.

Finally, the Virginia Company, an organization of merchants and wealthy men in England chartered by King James I to settle the New World, offered a possible solution. A new colony desperately needed laborers. The company would pay the costs of transportation to America in return for travelers' labor when they arrived. Newcomers would even receive free land at the end of their service. Other merchants followed suit, hiring subcontractors to get prospective colonists to sign "indentures" agreeing to work a certain number of years in exchange for transportation to America. Unscrupulous agents plied prospective colonists with drink to get them to sign away their rights.

About half of all white immigrants to the English colonies during the seventeenth century were convicts or indentured servants. For some of these contract laborers, the risk paid off. They finished their period of service and became free farmers or workers. Others, however, met with harsh toil and broken promises. Those who spent their time "idly or unprofitably" could be sent to perform hard labor or whipped.

In the first half of the eighteenth century, the system of white indentured servitude tapered off. Plantation owners found black slaves from Africa to be a better bargain. These new slaves

12   Poverty: Public Crisis or Private Struggle?

could be purchased to work until they died. This brutal system of slavery would lay the foundation for the higher poverty levels among African Americans that persist to this day.

The "Deserving Poor" vs. "Paupers"

"A penny saved is a penny earned," US Founding Father Benjamin Franklin said in his famous maxim, expressing the popular wisdom of his day. Hard work kept people on the right path. Laziness bred poverty. Franklin disapproved of government welfare programs because he believed they took away "all inducements to industry, frugality, and sobriety." Every Sunday, ministers preached about the sins of idleness.

Still, they knew that not everyone could work. Paupers were whipped, auctioned off, and sent to workhouses. Charities and government relief, meanwhile, sprang up to serve those considered deserving of help. The ministers lauded charity for the sick, the infirm, orphans, widows, and others in need.

Colonists drew a firm line between the "deserving" and the "undeserving" poor. While they gave generously to those deemed unable to help themselves, they showed considerably less sympathy for the able-bodied poor they regarded as "paupers." As one theorist put it: "Pauperism is the consequence of wilful error, of shameful indolence, of vicious habits." An increase of pauperism in the early 1800s led to a new search for answers. Experts at the time saw a strong link between poverty and heavy drinking. In Massachusetts, for instance, one report concluded that, "of all the causes of pauperism, intemperance, in the use of spirituous liquors is the most powerful and universal."

Many communities established poorhouses (also called "alms-houses" and "poor farms"). At first, they seemed like a sensible alternative to doling out relief that could be abused by able-bodied

A Brief History of Poverty in America 13

The Progressive Era

Jane Addams and other reformers of the Progressive Era questioned the notion that poverty was synonymous with vice and laziness. Instead of blaming poverty on the individual, they argued that social and economic conditions were primarily responsible for the growing gap between rich and poor.

A pioneer in the new field of social work, Addams was born September 6, 1860. She grew up the daughter of a progressive-minded Illinois legislator and businessman who was a strong supporter of Abraham Lincoln. Even as a young child, Addams was shocked by the "horrid little houses" and garbage-strewn streets of Chicago. She identified with the victims of society because she, herself, felt like a misfit: a pigeon-toed little girl who suffered from a curvature of the spine.

After touring a mission for the poor in the slums of London, Addams founded Hull House in Chicago in 1889, launching the settlement-house movement in America. Instead of merely visiting the poor like traditional charity workers, she lived among them, bridging the gap between the classes. Hull House provided meaningful careers for a new generation of college-educated young women who became settlement workers. A proponent of women's suffrage, Addams viewed women as "civic housekeepers."

She and other reformers sponsored legislation to abolish child labor, establish juvenile courts, limit the hours of working women, and make school attendance mandatory. In 1912, the Progressive Party, headed by Theodore Roosevelt, supported many of these reforms as part of its platform.

However, after Addams failed to support World War I (1914–1918), her popularity faded. Reforms that seemed "praiseworthy before the

Poverty: Public Crisis or Private Struggle?

Jane Addams, who devoted her life to helping the poor and founded Chicago's Hull House, is pictured circa the 1870s.

war," said Addams, became "suspect" after it. With Addams discredited because she was seen as a radical, social workers saw less of a need to live in the neighborhoods they served. Calls for government involvement to supplement private charity fell on deaf ears.

vagrants. The institutions opened with the promise of reforming the morally flawed. Supervisors would ban both idleness and alcohol. Inmates would be kept busy farming their own food, weaving, and making tools.

However, the poorhouses failed to live up to their initial promise. Outdoor work tapered off in the winter. With operating costs kept low to act as a deterrent, poorhouses degenerated into institutions of mismanagement and squalor. Inmates stole liquor from the managers' private stock or bought it from corrupt employees. One report complained that the typical almshouse had become "a winter resort for tramps … a place where the drunkard and the prostitute" recuperated "between debauches."

By the 1850s, criticism of the workhouses led to the creation of new private charities and local government relief. The American Civil War brought the end of slavery for African Americans in 1865, but their economic opportunities would remain limited for decades (and in many ways, remain limited still). Meanwhile, the gap between the rich and the poor grew. New immigrants from Eastern Europe clustered in tenements in the great cities. Abandoned children ran wild in these breeding grounds of crime, disease, and despair.

Poverty During the Great Depression

Farmers suffered a decade-long depression in the 1920s, and low-skilled workers often found themselves out of work or with wages too low to support their families. Still, most people hailed the Roaring Twenties as a time of great prosperity. Sales of consumer goods boomed. The horse and buggy gave way to the automobile. Many people bought on credit and gambled on the stock market. Little did they know that the economic bubble was about to burst.

On Black Tuesday, October 29, 1929, the stock market crashed, triggering the worst depression in US history. Banks and businesses closed down. President Herbert Hoover, a strong believer in rugged individualism, underestimated the seriousness of the crisis. Calling the Depression a "temporary halt in the prosperity of a great people," he rejected calls for the federal government to provide relief to the fifteen million Americans affected (one-quarter of the workforce). Instead, he set forth a program of government aid to businesses. His efforts accomplished little.

Throughout the nation, out-of-work bankers stood in bread lines with unemployed laborers. The Great Depression deeply wounded the psyche of Americans who had long associated their self-worth with their work. Many unemployed fathers left home, ashamed of being unable to support their loved ones. Children, too, took off so as not to burden their families.

With no jobs to support themselves, people lost their homes. The homeless built shacks of cardboard, scrap metal, packing boxes, and tarpaper in settlements they called "Hoovervilles" out of bitterness toward the president's failed policies. Local aid and private charity did not have the resources to deal with the needs of the impoverished.

In 1932, the American people voted for change by electing Franklin Delano Roosevelt president in a landslide victory. President Roosevelt quickly set in motion his plan for a so-called New Deal. The US Congress approved a sweeping Works Progress Administration (WPA), which put millions of people to work in both blue-collar and white-collar jobs. In addition, Congress passed the Social Security Act, establishing a payroll tax to provide benefits for retirees and others in need. The law created a welfare program known as Aid to Dependent Children. President Roosevelt signed the Social Security Act on August 14, 1935.

The Great Depression ended with the start of World War II and the creation of military-related jobs. The late 1940s and 1950s

A Brief History of Poverty in America 17

ushered in another era of prosperity bolstered by the passage of the GI Bill in 1944. Anyone who had served in the military could take advantage of government assistance for college tuition and a home mortgage. As a result, in the 1950s, suburban areas (or "suburbs") throughout the United States expanded.

Not everyone, however, benefited from the new prosperity. In 1962, the publication of Michael Harrington's groundbreaking book, *The Other America*, focused new attention on poverty in the land of plenty.

Welfare Regulations and Safety Nets

In an address to Congress on March 16, 1964, President Lyndon B. Johnson declared a war on poverty:

> *Today we are asked to declare war on a domestic enemy which threatens the strength of our nation and the welfare of our people. If we now move forward against the enemy—if we can bring to the challenges of peace the same determination and strength which has brought us victory in war—then this day and this Congress will have won a secure and honorable place in the history of the nation and the enduring gratitude of generations of Americans yet to come.*

President Johnson's initiative set in motion a series of bills creating programs such as Head Start, food stamps, work-study, Medicare, and Medicaid, all of which still exist today. New provisions strengthened Social Security, reducing poverty among the elderly. The civil rights movement of the 1960s brought new legislation to end racial discrimination. However, as urban riots and the Vietnam War grabbed headlines, support for Johnson's

Great Society faded. Because of a lack of funding, the programs proved to be not so much a war on poverty as a skirmish.

In 1967, presidential candidate Robert F. Kennedy saw with his own eyes how poor people lived. Touring the Mississippi Delta, he stopped to chat with impoverished African American children who resided in windowless shacks. Americans reacted with shock upon seeing TV images of these children, whose bellies were distended from malnutrition. Kennedy's supporters suffered a major blow when he was assassinated shortly after midnight on June 5, 1968. Old problems lingered, and new issues surfaced.

In his book, *Losing Ground: American Social Policy 1950–1980*, Charles Murray described how an era of unprecedented social reform gave rise to unexpected consequences. Old welfare policies regarded by many critics as overly harsh gave way to more flexible policies, prompting a 125 percent increase in caseloads between 1965 and 1970. Murray argued that the new welfare regulations did a disservice to the poor by making it profitable to make short-term choices that would be destructive in the long run. Murray used the example of "Harold and Phyllis," a hypothetical young couple of unspecified race, to illustrate how people's behavior changed in response to shifts in government policy.

In Murray's scenario, Harold and Phyllis have just graduated from an average public school in an average American city when Phyllis becomes pregnant. In 1960, harsh regulations prevented women from receiving benefits if they had "a man in the house," and also ensured women would lose out on benefits if they got jobs to support themselves. So, instead of going on welfare, the couple probably would have gotten married and scraped by on their earnings. If Harold was lucky, he'd move up from his job operating the steam-presses in a laundry to driving the company's delivery truck to finding a unionized truck-driving job. However, by 1970, the rules had changed, and the new regulations made it logical for Phyllis to go on welfare and not get married. Harold probably

A Brief History of Poverty in America 19

During an anti-poverty investigation in 1967, Senator Robert F. Kennedy tours the Mississippi Delta to see how the poor live.

would work only sporadically in the laundry, finding little reason to search for something better. (Many have criticized this example for oversimplifying or ignoring many of the complex factors that influence human behavior and impact socioeconomic status.)

As time went on, unfounded and racist stereotypes of African American welfare recipients as "lazy" reduced public sympathy for the poor. President Ronald Reagan, for instance, talked about a "welfare queen" in Chicago with a mink coat and a Cadillac. When reporters searched for the real welfare recipient behind the story, they found that the woman accused of using eighty names and bilking the government out of more than $150,000 had actually used two aliases to collect much less: $8,000.

Conservatives such as Reagan were not the only people who saw problems with the welfare system. As the economy faltered, questions swirled about the government's aid to the poor. Had the expansion of the Aid to Families with Dependent Children program (a successor to the Aid to Dependent Children program of 1935) made it too easy for people to

A Brief History of Poverty in America   21

just live off the government? Was the government creating a new culture of welfare dependency?

Ending "Welfare as We Know It"

In 1992, Bill Clinton campaigned for the presidency on a promise to "end welfare as we know it." Once in office, President Clinton proposed a plan to replace welfare with work, bolstered by supportive services. Congress modified his plan to trim costs. In 1996, Clinton signed the Personal Responsibility and Work Opportunity Reconciliation Act (PRWORA). This measure replaced Aid to Families with Dependent Children with Temporary Assistance to Needy Families (TANF). The new program, which included an education and training component, set temporary limits and a five-year lifetime cap on welfare assistance. States could exclude certain groups (such as parents of children under a year old and disabled adults) from work requirements.

Has the welfare reform act of 1996 accomplished its goal of transforming "the culture of poverty"? Experts say the results have been mixed. The number of welfare cases decreased by more than 60 percent between 1994 and 2002. While employment rose, many left welfare to work in low-wage jobs. Meanwhile, more jobs moved to the suburbs, creating problems of accessibility for urban residents.

In 2005, Hurricane Katrina focused new awareness on the problems of the impoverished living on the margins of society. The majority of those trapped in New Orleans could not escape because they had no cars, no surplus money, and no place to go. Hurricane Katrina also drew attention to the problems of racial isolation and highly concentrated poverty.

Years later, the plight of the poor persists. The 2006 reauthorization of PRWORA required states to impose stricter work requirements. The new regulations raised the work-participation rates that states must meet from 50 percent of families with an adult receiving TANF assistance to 70 percent of such families by 2010. The law remains in effect.

Today, lawmakers are increasingly targeting health care as a necessity whose high costs contribute to poverty. The Patient Protection and Affordable Care Act, signed into law in 2010 by President Barack Obama, sought to increase the number of Americans with health insurance coverage and thereby reduce the likelihood that single catastrophic health events, such as car accidents, could suddenly leave individuals or families with massive debts. According to one measure, health coverage reduced the US poverty rate by nearly one-quarter in 2014.

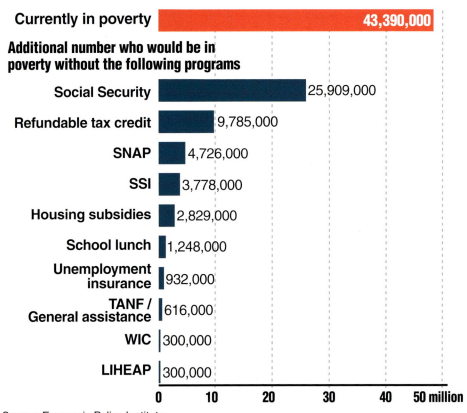

Chapter Two

HOW DOES POVERTY HAPPEN?

Millions of Americans live in poverty, but the conditions that create poverty can vary based on a number of factors, including class, race, geography, and education level. To arrive at better solutions, one must first understand how poverty happens.

The Poverty Line

Allison remembers exactly when she realized her family was poor. She was sitting at her desk in sixth grade, looking at the calculations on the blackboard. Her teacher had just told the class that some people in

Opposite: Tens of millions of Americans live in poverty, and millions more would without such programs as Social Security.

America live in the upper class, others in the middle class, and still others in poverty.

"I counted the kids in my family, looked at her figures and came to the shocking realization that my family lives at poverty level," Allison told *Teen People*. "I couldn't have a lot of stuff I wanted, but I never thought about it that way before."

Like Allison, more than forty million Americans live below the poverty line set by the US government, which in 2017 was $12,752 in annual wages for an individual and $25,283 for a family of four. Poverty affects people from all backgrounds, but some groups have higher rates than others. Here's a statistical snapshot of who lived below the official poverty line according to the 2016 census:

- *12.7 percent of all Americans*
- *8.8 percent of whites*
- *22 percent of African Americans*
- *19.4 percent of Hispanics*
- *26.2 percent of Native Americans*
- *26.8 percent of people with disabilities*
- *14 percent of women*

Clearly, factors such as race, ethnicity, country of origin, sex, and health ensure that different groups of people experience different poverty rates.

Some experts believe that the US government sets its poverty line too low. For one thing, fixed expenses such as rent have increased since the government developed its formula in 1964. For another, the government's calculations fail to account for debt such as credit-card balances and college loans. Each month, debt eats up a substantial chunk of family income. Since 1949, total debt as a percentage of disposable income has increased nearly fourfold, according to the Brookings Institution. Finally, many people live on the fringes of poverty. They make too much money to qualify for government assistance but not enough to get by.

Poverty hits people in the psyche as well as the wallet. Often, being broke makes people feel broken. The belief that anyone who works hard can make it in America stings for those who don't have enough money to pay the bills. Life doesn't seem fair. Many in poverty feel like they're playing a game without enough chips to win.

Being poor in America is different from living in poverty in the developing world. Someone from Somalia or Bangladesh might lack the running water, central heating, and cars that even America's poor can access. However, being poor in a land of plenty poses special challenges. People want what they see around them. In his book, *The Working Poor: Invisible in America*, David Shipler writes that the skills of surviving in poverty learned by people in poor countries have largely been lost in the United States.

"Visit a slum in Hanoi [Vietnam] and you will find children inventing games with bottles and sticks and the rusty rims of bicycle wheels," Shipler writes. "Go to a slum in Los Angeles and you will find children dependent on plastic toys and video games."

Social Class

Experts use the term "class" to describe groups of people in similar economic and social positions. Class is commonly described in terms of four criteria: education, income, occupation, and wealth.

At first, a person's class is his or her parents' class. It's as though everyone is dealt a hand of cards at birth, one from each suit: education, income, occupation, and wealth. Later, however, players may pick up new hands of their own. Bill Clinton, for

How Does Poverty Happen? 27

instance, began with "low" cards but emerged a winner thanks to a college education and a Rhodes scholarship.

In some ways, class differences have blurred over the years. "The old system of hereditary barriers and clubby barriers has pretty much vanished," said Eric Wanner, president of the Russell Sage Foundation, a social science research group in New York City. These days, it's harder than in the past to gauge class through material possessions, because factories around the world churn out low-priced consumer goods. Discount stores sell low-priced imitations of designer clothes and home furnishings.

However, in other ways, class divisions have deepened in recent years. The gap between the rich and poor has widened: the after-tax income of the top 1 percent of American households jumped 139 percent between 1979 and 2001, compared to just 17 percent for the middle fifth and only 9 percent for the poor. By 2015, the top 10 percent of American wage-earners made nine times as much money, on average, as the bottom 90 percent. The top 1 percent made forty times more, having "more than doubled their share of the nation's income since the middle of the 20th century," according to Inequality.org.

Class still plays a big role in determining who gets into which four-year college. Class differences also play an increased role in health, with Americans at the top of the class ladder

Journalist and author Ta-Nehisi Coates wrote an influential essay explaining why reparations for African Americans are key to fighting multigenerational poverty. The essay appeared in the *Atlantic* magazine in 2014.

How Does Poverty Happen? 29

living longer and maintaining better health than those at the bottom. Family structure differs considerably by class as well, with the educated and affluent more likely to have children while married. Because privileged couples typically also have fewer children, they're in a superior position to invest in them. Finally, more than in the past, the affluent are choosing to live apart from everyone else in gated communities and exurban mansions.

Race and Reparations

Although many African Americans have moved into the middle and upper classes, race continues to shape their experiences. A study released in 2018 points to racism, not class, as a primary motivator for the gap between whites and African Americans when it comes to economic success.

The study, conducted by Stanford University researchers, found that black boys raised in comparable households to those of white boys ultimately fare worse than whites in 99 percent of the country. As the *New York Times* explains, "White boys who grow up rich are likely to remain that way. Black boys raised at the top, however, are more likely to become poor than to stay wealthy in their own adult households."

In response to these findings, Ibram Kendi of the Antiracist Research and Policy Center at American University said: "One of the most popular liberal post-racial ideas is the idea that the fundamental problem is class and not race, and clearly this study explodes that idea." The few American neighborhoods where African American boys ultimately fared as well as whites "were the places where many lower-income black children had fathers at home," the *New York Times* elaborates. Given the high rate of incarceration among people of color, and African American men in particular, many argue that the study points to incarceration as one factor keeping Americans—and unfairly targeted minorities, especially—in poverty.

It's not just contemporary racism keeping African Americans and minorities from succeeding. While slaves of African descent were forced to work against their will in pre–Civil War America, whites were building family wealth, acquiring land, and starting businesses, all with the help of this labor for which slaves were never paid. Even after slavery was abolished, African Americans were systematically deprived of their property and denied opportunities to advance professionally and economically. For instance, a 2001 Associated Press investigation found that twenty-four thousand acres of land worth tens of millions of dollars had been stolen from more than four hundred African Americans since the antebellum period. The legacy of these thefts has kept the poverty rate among African Americans relatively high.

This is why many groups have called for reparations—funds to make amends for wrongs committed—to be paid to African Americans. In a 2014 essay for the *Atlantic*, Ta-Nehisi Coates outlines the case for reparations:

> *Perhaps no statistic better illustrates the enduring legacy of our country's shameful history of treating black people as sub-citizens, sub-Americans, and sub-humans than the wealth gap. Reparations would seek to close this chasm … Won't reparations divide us? Not any more than we are already divided. The wealth gap merely puts a number on something we feel but cannot say—that American prosperity was ill-gotten and selective in its distribution. What is needed is an airing of family secrets, a settling with old ghosts. What is needed is a healing of the American psyche.*

The United States has paid reparations in the past. During World War II, 117,000 people of Japanese descent—two out of three of whom were American citizens—were detained in internment camps under suspicion of collaborating with Japan in the attack on Pearl Harbor, Hawaii. However, in 1976, President Gerald Ford renounced the internments as a national mistake. In the 1990s, each living survivor was paid $20,000 in reparations. In an official letter, President George H. W. Bush wrote: "We can never fully right the wrongs of the past. But ... in enacting a law calling for restitution and offering a sincere apology, your fellow Americans have ... renewed their traditional commitment to the ideals of freedom, equality, and justice."

Upward Mobility

For generations, jobs in manufacturing have provided a stepping-stone from poverty into the ranks of the middle class. However, because many of these positions have been outsourced to lower-wage workers overseas, the working poor in the United States are increasingly working in service-sector positions in restaurants and stores, or in janitorial jobs.

For immigrants like Juan Manuel Peralta, the climb out of poverty can be particularly difficult. Peralta left Mexico at the age of nineteen to join his uncle in New York City. He expected to work hard and rise out of poverty. However, fifteen years later, that had yet to happen.

As an undocumented immigrant, he bounced from one restaurant job to another, married at the age of twenty-five, started a family, and eventually landed a job in the kitchen at 3 Guys, an upscale Greek restaurant in New York City. However, a combination of personal factors and work-related challenges held him back. Peralta's schedule at 3 Guys changed from week to week, making it impossible to count on a secure salary. Also, he sent part of his earnings back home to Mexico.

At 3 Guys, Peralta acquired a reputation as a hothead because he sometimes argued with waiters. Tensions flared between the predominantly Greek servers and the lower-paid Mexican kitchen workers. Only one Mexican, who happened to look Greek, had been promoted to the position of server. After Peralta and other Mexicans brought their grievances to the Restaurant Opportunities Center, a workers' rights group, the owners promised to promote a Mexican worker to server within a month. By the time the owners promoted a Mexican busboy ten months later, Peralta had been fired. (He denied his boss's contention that he was not a good worker.)

After his stint at 3 Guys, Peralta went to work as a grill cook at a diner in Queens. His schedule, though, kept changing, and he found himself arguing with the owner. One of those disagreements prompted him to leave and get a new job. Despite his setbacks, Peralta was still earning more money in the United States than he would be in Mexico—though not enough to move out of poverty. His experiences show how difficult it can be to find upward mobility.

Manufacturing jobs plummeted during and after the Great Recession of 2007–2009, but by 2018 they were steadily climbing back up.

The Missing Class

Valerie Rushing moved up from poverty to the next rung on the socioeconomic ladder. After years of working low-wage jobs, the thirty-three-year-old African American single mother had landed a $13.68-an-hour janitorial job with the Long Island Rail Road. Her new position (complete with full benefits)

Immigration Policy and Poverty

Twenty-year-old Arizona State University student Manuel Espinoza-Vazquez was facing the possibility of deportation after making an improper right turn. When the police officer asked for his license, Espinoza-Vazquez produced a Mexican ID. The officer transported him to the Immigration and Customs Enforcement (ICE) office in Phoenix, Arizona. "I'm scared," Espinoza-Vazquez told the *Arizona Republic* at the time. "I just want to graduate."

Supporters of broad-based rights for immigrants maintain that they do the hard work most native-born Americans don't want to do. Critics of such policies, on the other hand, point to the strain immigration puts on taxpayer-funded services. However, legal immigrants must wait five years to access such benefits, and undocumented immigrants are never legally allowed to do so. In fact, the poverty rate for immigrants in the United States in 2015 was only slightly higher than the rate for the American-born population.

While new immigrants lack the education levels of native-born Americans, many immigrant families become more educated and financially secure over time. Their initial standard of living might be lower than that of native-born Americans, but compared to life in their countries of origin, they're generally better off. Their children experience more upward mobility than the average native-born American.

So what's to be done? Proposals to reform immigration range from stricter limits and harsher penalties for the undocumented to strategies to help them obtain legal work and citizenship. Under the Barack Obama presidential administration, federal enforcers focused on deporting criminals and people who had recently crossed the border illegally. "Today's immigrants seek to follow in the same tradition of immigration

Immigrant farm worker Humberto doesn't have the money to pay for rent, so he is homeless, and camps with fellow workers.

that has built this country. We do ourselves and them a disservice if we do not recognize the contributions of these individuals," Obama argued.

However, President Donald Trump has called for a US-Mexico border wall, a decrease in legal immigration, and an end to such policies as "chain migration," which allows immigrants' families to join them in the United States. All of these policies, he argues, will not only protect national security but increase wages and employment for US-born workers.

How Does Poverty Happen?   35

helped her leave behind her old life of minimum-wage jobs as a childcare worker, shoe-store employee, and fast-food cashier.

Her story, profiled by authors Katherine S. Newman and Victor Tan Chen in their highly acclaimed book, *The Missing Class: Portraits of the Near Poor in America*, illustrates how difficult it can be for the near-poor to hold onto their hard-won victories. Newman and Chen coined the term "the missing class" to describe the roughly sixty million people who live in households that earn roughly $20,000 to $40,000 a year. The near-poor are rarely on the nation's radar screen. Newman and Chen wrote their book to shine the spotlight on these Americans who generally earn too much to qualify for government assistance.

Rushing supported two children—her daughter, Akeelah, and her sister's son, Johnny. The boy's crack-addicted grandmother and unreliable mother had left him in her care. Rushing and the two children lived in a $700-a-month apartment in Brooklyn, New York.

Like many people in the missing class, Rushing's life changed dramatically with the fortunes of her extended family. The reappearance of Yamika, Johnny's mother, made things harder for Valerie. Yamika promised Johnny visits and gifts that never came. Bitterly disappointed, the boy started acting out in class. Rushing let Yamika move in with her on the condition that she contribute a modest $25 a week and look after Johnny. Yamika failed to live up to her end of the bargain. Finally, Rushing told her sister she'd have to leave in another two months.

Two years later, Newman and Chen found Rushing a changed woman. Her entire disposition seemed more cheerful. Yamika and Johnny had both moved out. Although Johnny was still misbehaving, his mother was finally ready to be a better parent. Valerie had moved to a larger apartment in Brooklyn.

Looking back on the burden of taking care of Johnny, she said, "I did it because that was my nephew. I didn't want to see him in the system." Still, it had taken a toll on her. "Now that I can see what I can do on my own time by myself, I don't want to start over."

Rushing's story echoes those of many who struggle to make a better life for their children. Her future, and those of many others, will undoubtedly depend on the complex interactions between individual and societal responsibility. In the end, a multitude of factors determines a person's economic success or failure in the United States, but just as individual responsibility can't be ignored, social and political contributors to poverty can't, either.

Chapter Three

FAMILIES IN POVERTY

Few Americans exhibit the signs of extreme hunger—skeletal frames and distended bellies—common in the developing world. However, many still suffer from hunger. Many of those who qualify for government assistance use up their food stamps before the end of the month because of the high cost of groceries. Others make too much money to qualify for food stamps but not enough to pay their bills and put food on the table—in fact, 58 percent of food-insecure Americans live in households whose income exceeds the poverty line. Both groups turn to charitable organizations that are having trouble keeping up with the growing demand for food. Researchers call the condition of being unable to buy enough groceries to last the month "food insecurity."

Opposite: Two-year-old Aliyan Brooks lives with her parents and siblings in a homeless shelter in Orange County, California.

Families in Poverty   39

This challenge is just one of many that Americans living below the poverty line must face.

Food Insecurity

More than forty million Americans face problems with hunger—almost as many people as those living below the poverty line. This is due to a variety of factors. For instance, because so few supermarket chains remain in the inner cities, many poor urban families are forced to rely on expensive mom-and-pop stores. Snacks and fast foods with little nutritional value abound in these neighborhoods. As a result, some people are both obese and food-insecure.

Gladys, a retiree in Seattle, Washington, spent 70 percent of her income on rent. After paying her bills, she had little money left for food. Like many senior citizens, she had health problems that required a special diet. However, she didn't have a car, and without access to transportation, she couldn't get to the big supermarkets that offered the best prices and selections. Instead, she shopped at a little convenience store in her neighborhood.

"I can get very little with my money there," she said. "Most of the time I can't eat what I get at the food bank because my doctor wants me to follow a very strict diet. I have very high blood pressure and I'm also battling cancer, so I am supposed to eat a lot of vegetables and fruit. Those are very expensive and I am able to buy them very rarely."

Among those who suffer from food insecurity are 5.4 million seniors like Gladys and thirteen million children. That's one in six children in the United States. Many rely on programs that allow them to access reduced-price or free meals at school, but five in six of these children aren't getting free meals during the summer, when school is out of session.

One program designed to help people and families suffering from food insecurity is the Supplemental Nutrition Assistance Program, or SNAP. Twenty million US children rely on this program—and forty-five million Americans in total. SNAP not only helps low-income families pay for food, it also assists families who have been negatively impacted by natural disasters or economic downturns. A similar federal program, the Special Supplemental Nutrition Program for Women, Infants, and Children (WIC), is focused on helping children younger than five and women who are breastfeeding or pregnant. More than half of all babies born in the United States benefit from this program.

Teen Pregnancies

Rebecca watched the pink "X" appear on the dipstick.

She was pregnant. Another teenage mother without the income to care for a child. At first, she was shocked and terrified at what the future might hold. Slowly, she warmed to the idea of creating a new family with her boyfriend—but a few months later, they broke up. She gave birth and, with the help of supportive relatives and teachers, finished high school. She grew up alongside her baby.

Life proved to be harder than she had expected. With bills to pay for the first time, Rebecca needed to go on welfare. Eventually, she landed a position as a paralegal trainee and got married, but she regrets that, as a teen, she acted more like a big sister than a mother to her daughter.

"Take it from someone who has been there," she wrote in her first-person story, originally published in the *St. Petersburg Times*. "It's up to each sexually active teenager to learn to protect himself or herself."

Antipoverty experts echo Rebecca's sentiments. Becoming a single parent, particularly as a teenager, increases one's

Families in Poverty   41

chances of living in poverty because such families lack the financial cushion and resource pooling of two-wage-earner households. Many single mothers work long hours in low-wage jobs and are unable to afford quality childcare. Households with children are more likely to experience food insecurity, according to Feeding America, an organization that operates food banks throughout the country; 17 percent of households with children suffer from food insecurity compared with 11 percent of those without children. What's more, those with single heads of household—32 percent of households headed by single women and 22 percent headed by single men—are more likely to experience this kind of insecurity.

Teen pregnancy rates are decreasing. In fact, they were down 9 percent between 2015 and 2016, according to the Centers for Disease Control and Prevention (CDC)—and 51 percent between 2007 and 2016. Still, cases like Rebecca's are common. Although she did not plan to get pregnant, she didn't take action to prevent a pregnancy, either. Often, teens blame their pregnancies on "bad luck" or say that it "just happened." Some see their pregnancy as a ticket to adulthood in neighborhoods that offer few other opportunities.

Growing up in poverty and growing up in a single-parent family increase a teenager's risk of becoming pregnant. After giving birth, the financial challenges continue. Just 50 percent of teen mothers graduate from high school by age twenty-two, compared to 90 percent of women who have not given birth as a teenager. This lack of education narrows a young mother's career and economic opportunities, and makes it more likely that she and her child will grow up in poverty. After all, in 2016, the typical college graduate earned 56 percent more than people with high school diplomas—and those without the latter earned even less.

The CDC reports that in 2010—the latest year for which data was available—$9.4 billion in taxpayer money went to pay for the health care and foster care needs associated with teen pregnancy and childbirth. These funds were also spent toward the increased incarceration rates common among the children of teen parents, who also tend to do less well in school, have a higher dropout rate, and even suffer more health problems.

Because it's easier and more effective to prevent teen pregnancy than to deal with the negative social and economic consequences of such births, policymakers have made prevention a top priority. Researchers attribute much of the decreasing teen pregnancy rate

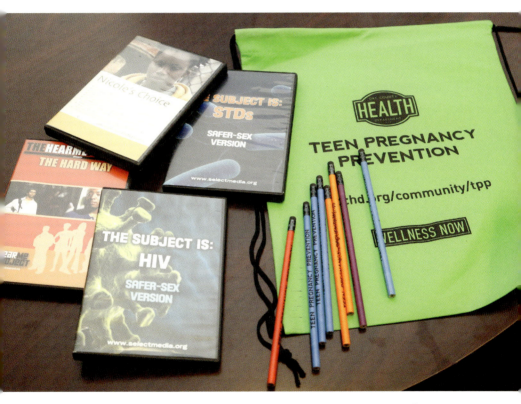

These materials are used in the program to prevent teen pregnancy by the Oklahoma City County Health Department.

Families in Poverty

to better use of contraception, and better access to it thanks to the Patient Protection and Affordable Care Act, which came into full effect in 2014, and which ensured affordable contraception for women. They also speculate that new child-support provisions may be prompting young men to think twice before engaging in unprotected sex.

However, the so-called "abstinence wars" could stall future progress. Battle lines have formed over how best to teach sex education in public schools. In one camp are those who support teaching teens to be abstinent until marriage. In the other camp are advocates for comprehensive sexuality education, which includes contraception.

Research shows that students who take a "virginity pledge" as part of abstinence-only programs are just as likely to get pregnant or develop sexually transmitted diseases as nonpledgers. To break the deadlock over the abstinence wars, the Society for Adolescent Medicine has recommended a comprehensive approach that includes abstinence education as well as the correct and consistent use of condoms for teens that choose to be sexually active.

Many experts believe that sex education is not enough; adolescents also need to see a brighter future. Programs such as Girls Inc. try to prevent teen pregnancy by giving students candid information about sexuality and providing after-school activities and mentors.

Seventeen-year-old Erika, for instance, decided that she didn't want to follow the same path as her best friend, Maria, who got pregnant in high school. Although Maria tried to keep up with school through independent study, she found herself unable to balance schoolwork with the demands of parenting. Erika, on the other hand, began attending Girls Inc. and decided to go to college. "You can't sugarcoat things like teen pregnancy and teen motherhood," she wrote.

Household Structure and Poverty

In the 1950s, girls like Maria and Rebecca often married the fathers of their children. The stigma of out-of-wedlock births sent many teenage girls scurrying to the altar for "shotgun weddings." The 1960s heralded a cultural revolution that called for individual freedom. The old taboos against divorce and single parenting lost much of their sway. At around the same time, the loss of manufacturing jobs spelled economic uncertainty for many unskilled workers. Financial stresses took a toll on couples, making some reluctant to get married and others more prone to divorce.

The "traditional" American family consisting of two married, heterosexual parents has increasingly given way to single-parent households, cohabitation, blended families, and households headed by LGBTQ and same-sex parents who only a few years ago were declared legally able to marry in all fifty states. In fact, just 46 percent of children live in so-called traditional households today.

Concern about how single-parent families affect children has long provoked controversy. Are single parents responsible for their own economic plight, or should society do more to help? In 1965, the question divided supporters from critics of a report written by then–assistant secretary of labor Daniel P. Moynihan, lamenting the rise of single motherhood in poor urban communities. Even though the report blamed the trend on rising male unemployment and called on the federal government to play a more active role in ensuring jobs for African American men, critics of the Moynihan Report accused it of "blaming the victim."

However, since then, an extensive body of research has shown that family formations have decidedly public consequences. Children raised by two parents generally do better than those

Families in Poverty   45

in other types of households. That's not to say, however, that children from single-parent families are doomed. Many do very well indeed. However, on average, children who grow up with only one biological parent (it's usually the mother) are more likely to develop behavioral problems, drop out of school, and end up in poverty than children from two-parent households.

Economic problems account for a large portion of the negative outcomes, according to sociologist Sara McLanahan. Children in two-parent households (and, to a lesser extent, cohabiting families) benefit from pooled resources and because, if both work, there is more money coming in. However, economics alone do not tell the full story. Because single parents do not have a partner with whom to share responsibilities, they cannot give their children as much time and attention as two parents can. Low parental involvement, supervision, and aspirations, as well as greater residential mobility, contribute to the negative outcomes of children growing up with only one parent.

McLanahan uses the term "fragile families" to describe these households. A large percentage of the relationships between single mothers and the fathers of their children end by the time the baby is five. Often, these women form new partnerships resulting in more children. While cohabitation and remarriage might increase income, they usually do not bring as many benefits as primary marriages.

Financial dealings in these fragile families are often rife with tension, researchers say. Should the mother's new boyfriend pay for sneakers for a child? Will a man jeopardize his relationship with his new wife if he gives money to a child from a previous relationship? Married parents who are poor break up at a higher rate than nonpoor parents. Meanwhile, many couples fearful of divorce put off marriage until they feel emotionally and financially secure. For some, that day never comes.

Can Money Buy Happiness?

Researcher Dan Buettner has traveled the world to see where people are the happiest. Using results from elaborate questionnaires given to hundreds of thousands of men and women around the globe, Buettner points to Denmark as one of the happiest places on earth.

Denmark is hardly the tropical paradise one might associate with happiness. Still, people there report high levels of contentment. The United States ranked twenty-third on the list, well behind Switzerland, Austria, Iceland, and the Bahamas. Impoverished countries in Asia, on the other hand, have particularly low levels of happiness, with China and India low on the list.

The Danes pay some of the highest taxes in the world but the government spends more money per capita on children and the elderly than any other country. People describe themselves as feeling "tucked in," like a snug child.

"They have this thing called 'Jante-lov,' which essentially says, 'You're no better than anybody else,'" Buettner explained. "A garbage man can live in a middle-class neighborhood and hold his head high."

Adrian White, an analytic social psychologist, produced the first-ever "world map of happiness." From analyzing a number of studies, he found a nation's level of happiness is most closely associated with health levels, followed by wealth and educational opportunities.

Studies show a strong correlation between poverty and unhappiness. Once people are able to get their basic needs met, they become much happier. However, beyond that, money doesn't make much difference, researchers say. While an American who earns $50,000 a year is apt to be twice as happy as someone who earns $20,000 a year, the payoff for surpassing $90,000 is slight. More money at this level can lead to more stress.

Families in Poverty

Human and Social Capital

Experts see upward mobility in terms of both an individual's capabilities and his or her social supports. According to the *New York Times*, sociologists use the terms "human capital" and "social capital" to describe the twin pillars of success. Human capital refers to a person's education, job credentials, and employability. Social capital refers to a person's emotional support from a reliable stakeholder in one's life, an asset commonly associated with marriage.

Often, single mothers lack both kinds of capital. For three years, author Sharon Hays visited the homes of welfare offices and welfare clients to research her book *Flat Broke with Children: Women in the Age of Welfare Reform*. Hays found several common patterns among the welfare clients she interviewed, including a domino effect of personal tragedy and the inconsistent use of birth control. These clients also tended to feel conflicting forces both pushing them to work and pulling them to be at home with their children or families.

Consider the case of "Sheila," a twenty-nine-year-old white woman identified by a pseudonym for reasons of confidentiality. Sheila's downward spiral began after her high school sweetheart was killed in an auto accident. Instead of going to college as planned, she took a part-time job and spent much of her time "sitting and mourning and moping and weeping." Then, her father left her mother. Shortly afterward, her mother developed blood clots in her legs, which made it impossible for her to work. Sheila lost her job, and she and her mother became homeless.

While homeless, Sheila met Sam, a man she saw as her savior because he let her and her mother move in with him. Sheila became pregnant, but Sam, who was secretly married, left. Homeless again, Sheila was raped. She went on welfare, which

Carolina Fuentes, twenty-two, and her five-year-old daughter hope to sign up for financial help and food stamps at a California welfare office.

allowed her to get a small studio to live in with her mother, who watched Sheila's daughter while Sheila took a string of temporary or low-paying jobs. Her luck seemed to turn for the better when she worked her way up to a management position in a fast-food restaurant. However, because the hours and the bus rides were so long, she quit that job. Whether she'd be able to find a more flexible position remained to be seen.

The Marriage Movement

Researchers who study people who have pulled themselves out of poverty into the ranks of the middle class point to the importance of work and marriage. But is marriage a realistic goal for the majority of single mothers?

Many experts say no. "Women who have children [from other relationships] are the least likely to find a mate," McLanahan said. One PBS Frontline special, "Let's Get Married," profiled twenty-eight-year-old Ashaki, a single mother of seven on welfare. At the time, Ashaki was wrestling with the question of whether or not to marry her boyfriend, Steven, the father of her youngest child. Frontline met up with Ashaki at Family Focus, one of a growing number of programs that teach relationship skills to unmarried couples with children. Agencies typically approach unmarried couples at the "magic moment," the time around the birth of a child, when hopes and dreams soar. Relationship-skills classes typically address topics such as financial management and conflict resolution. In 2006, Congress allocated $750 million over five years for these programs to promote "healthy marriages" and "responsible fatherhood."

The Bush administration advocated the promotion of healthy marriages as a way to fight poverty and aid children. "You see, strong marriages and stable families are incredibly good for children," said then-president George W. Bush, "and stable families should be the central goal of American welfare policy." President Barack Obama also pushed for strong, two-parent families.

However, critics of the marriage movement argue that couples need resources such as decent-paying jobs and childcare before they can consider tying the knot. In areas plagued by high rates of incarceration, unemployment, mental health problems, and violence, a woman might have a child with a man but not regard him as marriage material.

Ashaki was a case in point. "I thought about marrying my oldest daughter's father," she told Frontline, "but we spent like ten years in and out of a relationship. He was kind of crazy. Violent, really."

Steven, on the other hand, won her over by helping with her children. He took them to school and to the park. He even taught the five oldest children a dance routine to the Temptations song

50 Poverty: Public Crisis or Private Struggle?

"My Girl." Ashaki lived in an apartment, which for weeks had no gas. She had to cook on a hot plate. Her relationship with Steven, though, blossomed. "You know, we just seem so right together," she said. "When I'm with him, it's like, this is my soulmate. And I think that's why I want to marry him."

However, Ashaki wanted certain things to be in place before getting married. She hoped for Steven to have a job. Steven, though, had trouble finding employment. To help Ashaki pay for milk and diapers, he sold drugs. When he was caught, he was sentenced to three months in boot camp. Ashaki put the marriage on hold. One of her daughters was so heartbroken, she drew a picture of the engagement ring Ashaki had pawned as a plea for the couple to stay together.

Whether relationship classes can help couples like Ashaki and Steven develop stable marriages remains to be seen. Many experts believe that such programs will have the best chance of success if they're linked to other supports, such as employment and mental-health services.

In the end, there's no single type of family ideal for raising children and rising above the poverty line. Still, the role of government, nonprofits, and public education in preventing poverty for families and children remains up for debate. What approach works best is likely to vary from family to family.

Chapter Four

THE SUBURBAN POOR

The suburbs are experiencing the greatest increase in poverty of any type of community in the nation. "Suburbs in the country's largest metro areas saw the number of residents living below the poverty line grow by 57 percent between 2000 and 2015. Altogether, suburbs accounted for nearly half (48 percent) of the total national increase in the poor population over that time period," Elizabeth Kneebone of the Brookings Institution reported in 2017. How has this happened? Many complex factors, including the Great Recession of 2007–2009 and an increase in low-wage work, have contributed to this trend.

Shifting Geographies

Christopher Gale hated going back to school after the winter break.

Opposite: Many Americans lost their homes because of the foreclosure crisis that began in 2007.

The Suburban Poor   53

"Everyone else seemed to have everything, and we had nothing," he said. "My mom did her best. But it was awful going back to school after Christmas and seeing everyone's toys."

In suburbs like Christopher's, the "have-nots" brush up against the "haves" every day. The former flip burgers and bag groceries to help their families while the latter buy expensive clothes and vacation in Paris. Some low-income suburbanites get the message they don't belong and feel that they have to hide their lack of money. Ada Estrella, for instance, pretended to live at a friend's house so her dates wouldn't have to drop her off at the Rolling Meadows trailer park, where she really lived. People in town called the park "Rolling Ghettos."

No longer are the suburbs the pristine retreat from urban ills depicted in 1950s sitcoms. Since then, the suburbs have changed. Communities once known for their basketball courts and manicured lawns have become sprinkled with boarded-up houses. During the Great Recession, real-estate deals that seemed too good to be true proved to be just that. The downwardly mobile often point to some combination of a lost job, family breakup, and health problem that pushed them over the edge.

In recent years, the geographic locale of poverty has shifted. While in 1999 the majority of people below the poverty line lived in inner cities, by 2015, just 19.6 percent of the poor lived in big cities, while 11.2 percent lived in the suburbs.

What accounts for this shift? Researchers point to several trends. First, jobs increasingly have moved from central cities to the suburbs. Second, immigrants are moving directly to the suburbs, bypassing the major cities altogether—though the US-born are still driving this poverty trend. Third, gentrification of urban neighborhoods has forced some low-income residents to surrounding suburbs. Fourth, the foreclosure crisis of the recession struck the suburbs hard. And fifth, the fastest-growing job sectors in the country are in low-income jobs, such as retail sales, that are more likely to be concentrated in the suburbs.

Being poor in the suburbs is a mixed bag. On the one hand, the suburbs offer some advantages over the inner cities. Because poverty is more hidden and dispersed than in inner cities, the suburban poor are less likely to live in neighborhoods overcome by poverty-related crime and drug abuse.

However, the suburbs also pose certain disadvantages. For one thing, cars are practically required, particularly in the outlying areas, because of spotty public transportation. Often people carpool to get to food pantries and soup kitchens that are scurrying to keep up with the rising demand for their services. At a soup kitchen in Hempstead, New York, for instance, manager Jean Victor used to make twenty pounds of pasta for lunch and have some left over. "Now we make 60 pounds, and there's none left over," she told a reporter.

Suburbs vary greatly from one another. While the rich suburbs are getting richer, the poor suburbs are getting poorer. A growing number of suburbs suffer from the same poor schools, crime, and drug abuse long linked to the inner city. Some observers call it the "urbanization of the suburbs."

"Throwaway" Neighborhoods

Growing up in Chelsea, Massachusetts, Jay Ash got used to the smells. First, there was the stench of burnt rubber from the neighborhood rubber plant. Then came the exhaust fumes from the trucks. Finally, Ash remembers the stink of the oil tanks that always prompted his dad to yell, "Roll up your windows!"

Such memories belie the popular notion of the suburbs as an idyllic place where birds chirp and flowers bloom. Once a summer resort for Boston's aristocracy, tiny Chelsea sprouted factories during the Industrial Revolution. Immigrants poured in, using

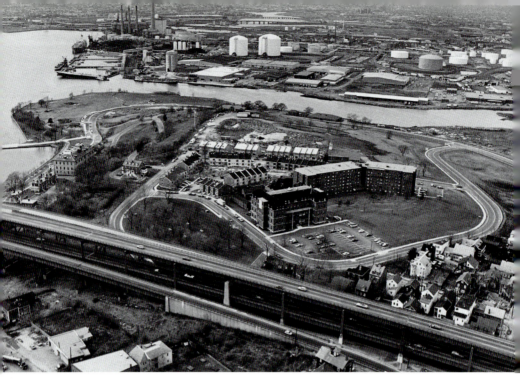

A housing project in Chelsea, Massachusetts, is pictured under construction in 1984.

Chelsea as a stepping-stone. "It was a close-knit neighborhood," Ash recalled when he was in his forties. "You looked out for your neighbors, and, if you had problems, your neighbors were looking out for you as well."

Chelsea became what experts call a "first-tier suburb," an outgrowth of the nearby big city. Like residents of other first-tier suburbs, the immigrants of Chelsea worked hard so they could move their families to the more prosperous outlying towns. In the process, they left behind a decaying infrastructure and houses in need of repair.

"The deterioration we observed … serves as an indictment of the 'throwaway' mentality that seems to dominate our culture: build it, use it, exploit it, abandon it," author William Hudnut wrote in his book, *Halfway to Everywhere: A Portrait of America's First-Tier Suburbs*. "In our consumer-oriented, disposal-minded society, houses, shops, neighborhoods, entire communities all go through an evolution that can end with a whimper."

Ash went away to college but returned to Chelsea in 1983 to become its city manager, an appointed position. The demographics of the neighborhood continued to change as people came and left. Factories closed down. While young people in Ash's day engaged in fistfights and car thefts, the new generation lived in a world of drugs, guns, knives, and gangs. The city plunged into a financial crisis, leading to state receivership in 1991.

After Chelsea regained its financial autonomy in 1995, new plans called for sweeping improvements. Chelsea's schools developed a partnership with Boston University. The city began acquiring old factories with the plan of turning them into housing. New galleries opened up. Young professionals attracted by Chelsea's proximity to Boston bought lofts in buildings that once manufactured cardboard boxes.

Still, poverty remains. As Ash saw it, this ethnically diverse community catered to first-generation immigrants who were bound to begin their lives in America relatively poor. Some new immigrants rise up the economic ladder, but not everyone can.

"Today it's more difficult to make that step up," Ash said.

Tensions over Immigration

In the primarily middle-class suburb of Farmingville, New York, two Mexican day laborers waited outside a convenience store one morning for their work assignments. Two white men pulled up, pretending to be contractors. Instead, they brought the two immigrants to an abandoned industrial park and attacked them with a post-hole digger and a knife. The laborers barely escaped with their lives. The two attackers were convicted of attempted manslaughter and sentenced to twenty-five years in prison.

This attack in a small Long Island town illustrates the growing resentment that some native-born Americans feel regarding the influx of immigrants in America's suburbs. Poverty exists not only in first-tier suburbs but also in surrounding towns, where new jobs have sprouted up in restaurants, strip malls, construction sites, and in the homes of well-heeled residents looking for gardeners and nannies. In these towns, affordable housing remains in short supply.

In Farmingville, a town of bungalows and ranch houses broken up by strip malls, day laborers and their families had crowded into tiny, single-family homes. Resentment toward immigrants had grown among suburbanites who worried that their property values were being jeopardized by overcrowding, increased traffic, and strained municipal services. Some townspeople even called day laborers "parasites" and threw rocks at them.

How authorities respond to complaints varies from suburb to suburb. In Farmingville, for instance, the police locked up eleven houses said to be dangerously overcrowded and evicted about two hundred tenants. The tenants, who were living in packed conditions some observers compared to the turn-of-the-century tenements, set up a tent city behind one of the houses in protest. In North Hempstead, New York, on the other hand, Nassau County officials helped tenants in overcrowded buildings find alternative housing. Tom Suozzi, the executive for Nassau County on Long Island, told *USA Today* that officials needed to find a delicate balance.

"Long-term residents have a legitimate concern that illegal housing is dangerous and devalues their neighborhoods," said Suozzi, the son of an Italian immigrant. "But day laborers and immigrant activists have a legitimate concern, also, that this issue cannot be used as an excuse for racism. So finding that balance is one of the tough challenges that exist."

Protesters stand up against presidential hopeful Donald Trump's comments linking immigrants to criminal activity in a 2015 protest.

While political leaders ponder plans for immigration reform, conflicts over immigration have pitted neighbor against neighbor, community against community. Some towns have passed exclusionary zoning to keep the people they employ in their homes, stores, and restaurants from moving into the community. In response, advocacy groups and local leaders who support immigrant rights have adopted the rallying cry, "If you're good enough to work here, you're good enough to live here."

Many observers attribute negative feelings toward immigrants to the middle class's growing fear of being squeezed by a tight economy. Some stressed-out suburbanites look for someone to blame for lower wages or lost employment opportunities. Experts, though, see this lack of economic opportunity as the real culprit.

"A strong middle class is the best ally of the poor," wrote Elizabeth Warren, then a professor at Harvard Law School. In 2012, Warren became a US senator. "A middle class that is rich with opportunity opens the paths out of poverty. A middle class that is financially strong can support the programs needed to give the poor a helping hand. A middle class that is prosperous provides the model for how education and hard work pay off."

Vacant Neighborhoods

Karen Volkman's neighborhood in Minnesota reflected the problems of a vanishing middle class. Fifteen years after Volkman, a postal worker, bought her modest home in 1993, her neighborhood had changed completely. Several houses were vacant, and empty lots stood where a bowling alley and jewelry store used to be.

"I'm not as happy with the neighborhood as when I bought it," Volkman told the *St. Paul Pioneer Press*. "People just don't take care of their stuff as much."

Boarded-up houses were signs of the foreclosure crisis besieging the nation at the height of the Great Recession. Since the 1970s, the number of Americans unable to pay their mortgages had increased fivefold. Home ownership had increasingly become a challenge for the middle-class and working-class residents who made up America's mainstream.

Maryanne Hernandez, for instance, bought her dream house in San Bernardino, California, in 2003. By 2007, she had fallen four months behind on her mortgage payments. "It's not just us," Hernandez told Reuters news service. "It's all over."

Analysts blamed much of the mortgage problem on the "sub-prime lending crisis." The term "sub-prime" refers to borrowers who have low credit ratings because they haven't paid their bills on time. Lenders had lured many prospective homeowners with poor credit by offering them attractive deals. The catch was that payments increased over time. Many borrowers gambled on themselves, thinking they could meet the payments, and lost.

By 2017, the US economy had recovered from the worst of the recession. Foreclosures were down 20 percent during the first six months of the year from the same period during 2016. Still, many prospective home-buyers still felt cautious, and some neighborhoods would never be the same.

Car Repossessions Speed Up

Life has been very good lately for the "repo man." That's a common nickname for people whose job is to repossess cars. In November 2017, more than six million Americans were at least ninety days late on paying their auto loans and were at risk of losing their vehicles. The delinquency rate had been steadily increasing since 2011.

"Some have started to compare what's happening in the auto loan market to the home mortgage crisis that helped trigger the Great Recession and financial crisis of 2008–2009," the *Washington Post* reported. "Many of the same issues are back: Lenders appear to have lowered their standards to give people car loans who probably should not qualify or should not be getting such a large loan."

As a result, owners can't keep up with their payments, so they end up on the radar of repo men. Stories of fights, confrontations, and shoot-outs with angry car owners who don't want to surrender their keys have dogged the repossession industry. But Kevin J. McGivern, president of Equitable Services Inc., a repo firm in Illinois, told a reporter he hasn't experienced any violent confrontations. "It's not a blood and guts business," he explained. "We do a lot of our repo business by talking to people first."

Sometimes the sight of the repo man is a relief. An owner tired of sinking money into skyrocketing gas rates and steep monthly payments might gladly turn over the car keys.

Many people who can't pay their car loans also have low credit scores, meaning that it will be hard for them to get a new car loan if they lose the vehicle they have. Because so many Americans rely on their cars to get to and from work every day, the loss of a car may result in a lost job and compounding financial troubles.

Daily Expenses

Where did all the money go? Have Americans frittered away all their disposable income on smartphones, video game systems, and other nonessentials? Not really, experts say. What's gone up—way up—are fixed expenses. Families in the twenty-first century pay considerably more for housing, health care, transportation, and childcare than their counterparts a generation ago. Warren outlined to the following changes between the early 1970s and the 2000s: the home mortgage had ballooned from $465 to $854 a month; families spent 74 percent more on health insurance; and overall transportation costs for a family of four had increased by 52 percent. A family with one preschooler and one child in elementary school in the 2000s paid an average of $1,048 a month for childcare compared to paying no childcare costs in the past, when one parent was more likely to be home full-time.

Often, to pay these bills, people trim food expenses and work extra jobs. In the 1970s, when a child was ill or a relative was sick,

In low-income households, careful budgeting is essential.

Poverty: Public Crisis or Private Struggle?

a family member could provide the care. Today, on the other hand, everyone is working. Many of the stressed-out, financially insecure middle-class families of the twenty-first century live paycheck to paycheck, sharing an uncertain future with the nation's poor.

Writing for the *Washington Post* in January 2018, Karen Weese pointed to the new fees and corporate policies that she said amounted to penalties for being poor. One woman, for instance, after paying her electricity bill late, was forced to pay a $250 "new customer" fee to have her electricity turned back on. Another example was Bank of America's newly announced change to its no-minimum checking accounts. Now, anyone falling below a $250 minimum monthly direct deposit or a $1,500 minimum daily balance would have to pay a monthly fee.

"The optics are breathtaking, considering Bank of America made more than $21 billion in profits last year and will receive a multibillion-dollar present from Congress every year from now on, courtesy of the newly slashed corporate tax rate. To celebrate their profits and congressional largesse by putting the squeeze on their poorest customers puts even more icing on their already well-iced cake," Weese wrote.

Chapter Five

THE URBAN POOR

The poverty rate reached historic highs during the Great Recession, and while it had only recently begun to recover by 2015, there were still 11.5 million more poor Americans than in 2000. Large cities were more likely to experience poverty than any other community in the United States, with a 19.2 percent poverty rate as of 2015, the latest year for which data was available in a 2017 Brookings Institution report. While more people of color are now moving to the suburbs, many point to a long history of racist political and economic policies at the root of poverty in urban areas, which still tend to be more diverse than suburban and rural communities. A complicated web of social and economic factors led to continued poverty in United States cities.

Opposite: The homeless live on the streets in tents and makeshift shelters in Los Angeles, California.

Race and Urban Poverty

In 2016, metropolitan areas had a 13.2 percent African American population and a 19.3 percent Hispanic population, compared to nonmetropolitan areas, which were 8.2 percent African American and 8.4 percent Hispanic. To talk about urban poverty, then, requires a discussion of how tightly intertwined issues of race and poverty can be.

In the case of African Americans in particular, a long history of slavery and institutionalized prejudice in the United States has contributed directly to their increased likelihood to be poor. Even after the abolishment of slavery, African Americans were prevented from owning property or obtaining loans to buy property or start businesses. They were denied entry into many public spaces and denied membership in unions, which advocate to improve pay and working conditions across a variety of industries. African Americans are more likely to be arrested than whites, and face longer sentences for the same crimes. Is America a land of opportunity or a nation that keeps African Americans trapped in a cycle of poverty?

In 2008, Barack Obama made history by becoming the nation's first African American president. Many voters wept with joy because they never thought they'd see the day when an African American would hold the country's highest office. Some argued that the election proved that change had come to America—that economic and other issues trumped race. However, the coming years would show that the war against racism still rages on today.

The rise of an exceptional individual like Obama, the son of a white woman from Kansas and a black man from Kenya, did not solve the problems of urban poverty or negate the existence of negative racial stereotypes. An Associated Press poll at the time found that one third of white respondents still agreed with at least one negative generalization of blacks. The stereotypes include that African Americans were "lazy," "violent," or responsible for their own troubles.

The years during and after Obama's presidency saw a slew of incidents in which law enforcement officers killed unarmed African Americans throughout the nation and faced few or no legal consequences. While these types of tragedies have occurred throughout the history of the United States, disproportionately affecting people of color, a slew of incidents filmed on smartphones and posted to social media stirred up new outrage. The 2014 shooting of an unarmed man, Michael Brown, in Ferguson, Missouri, sparked nationwide protests. A few months later, a twelve-year-old boy named Tamir Rice was playing with a toy gun when he was fatally shot by police. These and dozens of other incidents have sparked a movement called Black Lives Matter and proven that racism is still very much alive in America. Some now allege that President Donald Trump has—intentionally or not—reenergized a base of vocal white supremacists and made veiled racist comments himself.

Implicit Bias

In 2016, 22 percent of African Americans and 20 percent of Hispanic people lived in poverty compared to 9 percent of whites. Race remained inextricably linked to poverty and all the economic and social challenges that comes with it. So what can be done to dispel the racial stereotypes that so often contribute to this poverty?

First and foremost, experts say, individuals should recognize that everyone grows up with implicit racial biases, whether they are conscious of them or not. These biases can be modeled by adults or observed in the world, even in the form of subtle social cues or interactions. A famous experiment from the 1940s illustrated just how pervasive such biases were. Two psychologists showed seven dolls with different skin tones to children between the ages of three and seven. The children were asked which dolls they preferred. Most children, both black and white, preferred the white doll and associated positive characteristics such as beauty with that doll. "In other words," Eric Cooper explained in *HuffPost*, "Black children internalized the stereotypes they gleaned from growing up in a society that devalued them, discriminated against them and dismissed them as inferior."

New evidence shows that Americans still retain such biases, whether they mean to or not. A limited version of the doll study was performed again sixty years later on 133 children and yielded much the same results: "white children have an overwhelming white bias, and black children also have a bias toward white," reported CNN, which commissioned the study. Research from the Yale Child Study Center, released in 2016, showed that preschool staff and teachers held African American students to a higher standard of behavior, and "show a tendency to more closely observe Blacks and especially Black boys when challenging behaviors are expected." This may be why, although just 19 percent of preschoolers are African American, 48 percent of preschoolers who are suspended from school are African American.

Personal Responsibility and Institutionalized Racism

Many African American leaders—President Obama included—believe that, while the nation needs to fight prejudice, African Americans do have some control over their destinies. In a speech before the National Association for the Advancement of Colored People (NAACP), Obama said, "Now, I know there's some who've been saying I've been too tough talking about responsibility. But here at the NAACP, I'm here to report I'm not going to stop talking about it. Because—no matter how many ten-point plans we propose, or how many government programs we launch—none of it will make any difference if we don't seize more responsibility in our lives." Obama has insisted that African Americans can overcome some challenges by "demanding more from our fathers, and spending more time with our children, and reading to them, and teaching them that while they may face challenges and discrimination in their own lives, they must never succumb to despair or cynicism; they must always believe that they can write their own destiny."

However, others have argued that Obama did not take a strong enough stance in outlining the unique challenges and prejudices that African Americans faced during his presidency, even as the tragic deaths of innocent African Americans such as Michael Brown and Tamir Rice were being reported on the news. "Obama has and will always poll high among African Americans, but that should not be mistaken for blind support for him or the policies he champions," writes Keeanga-Yamahtta Taylor in the *Guardian* (UK). In fact, Taylor argues, Obama's election fed into the illusion of a post-racial America that simply didn't exist, and in many instances, the president took on the role of "informed observer" rather than vocal advocate for the African American community.

On the other hand, Obama's address to the NAACP did link civil rights to economic rights: "[I]t doesn't matter if you have the right to sit at the front of the bus if you can't afford the bus fare," he said. "It doesn't matter if you have the right to sit at the lunch counter if you can't afford the lunch."

While welfare reform has brought some gains to African American women and other groups, researchers say that poor African American men are being left behind. Studies by experts at Columbia, Princeton, and Harvard universities and at other institutions show that black males are more likely to drop out of school, experience joblessness, and face incarceration.

Barack Obama speaks at the NAACP convention on July 14, 2008, in Cincinnati, Ohio, during his first campaign for president.

"For almost as long as unemployment statistics have been recorded (since around the time of the Great Depression), a gulf has existed between white Americans and black and Hispanic Americans," wrote Gillian B. White in the *Atlantic* in January 2018. "A good yet unfortunate rule of thumb is that the unemployment rate for blacks is generally about twice as high as the one for whites." In December 2017, that gap had closed somewhat. Whereas 3.7 percent of white Americans were unemployed, 4.9 percent of Hispanics and 6.8 percent of African Americans were unemployed. "It's true that 6.8 percent is historically a fairly low unemployment rate for black Americans, but it's not a good or healthy unemployment rate by just about any measure," White explained.

The War on Drugs, launched by President Richard Nixon in 1971, has disproportionately impacted African Americans. Jonathan Rothwell, a senior economist at Gallup, reported in 2014 that even though whites are more likely to sell illicit drugs, African Americans are 3.6 times more likely to be arrested for selling drugs. And while the same percentage of African Americans and whites use illegal drugs, African Americans are 2.5 times more likely to be arrested for possessing illicit substances. African Americans also receive longer sentences on average for committing the same crimes. The result? About one in three African American males will, at some point in their lives, spend time in prison. This can have a direct impact on their own economic security and that of their families. Not only do incarcerated people lose out on years of income and job experience, many have a hard time finding work after they're released because few businesses want to hire people with prison records.

Meanwhile, urban areas experience more violence: in 2015, 81 percent of homicides involving a firearm occurred in urban areas, according to the CDC. The CDC also reports that African Americans are eight times more likely to be killed by a gun than white Americans. This could be in part attributable to the fact that the poor and poor minorities experience higher levels of unemployment and fewer economic opportunities overall, and therefore sometimes feel they have no choice but to participate in illegal activities such as selling drugs to survive. It might also be partly attributable to the unique type of poverty found in urban centers, which according to the Brookings Institution are more likely to have areas of concentrated poverty—that is, areas where large numbers of poor people live in one place. Such neighborhoods often have fewer high-quality jobs and opportunities for advancement, pushing more people toward desperate and sometimes dangerous means of survival.

Poverty Is "Contagious"

The housing development where Rachel lived was being torn down. Rachel (who was identified by her first name only) had a choice: she could either move to another housing project or use Section 8 vouchers to find an apartment on the private market.

Like most of the other people in her housing development, she chose the Section 8 option. She wanted a better environment for

A Difficult Journey

Carlos McBride's life story shows how the threads of personal and societal responsibility are often woven together. The son of a father who abused drugs and a mother who drank too much, Carlos dropped out of school after ninth grade and spent his days hanging out with his friends. He fathered two children out of wedlock and got his nickname "Rec" for being reckless. He took pride in his daring. Sometimes, he ran drugs from New York City to western Massachusetts.

In some ways, though, McBride's family defied the stereotype of the dysfunctional poor. His mother always cooked, and his father read books of philosophy. His grandmother looked after her big family, asking Carlos, who already had two children of his own, to take in his young cousin. "I know you're going to do something great," she told him.

Her faith in him planted a seed, but McBride wasn't yet ready to leave the streets. Even though he worked in a factory from seven at night until seven in the morning, he also felt the tug of the illegal economy. He told his father about his plans to carry out a small robbery. "I just want to tell you how much I love you," the elder McBride said. "Think about what you're doing."

His father's words began to take hold as the gun violence escalated. Carlos had lost one friend after another to death or prison. Finally, in his early twenties, a conflict with his landlady sent him to court. After he got probation, McBride decided to turn his life around. He entered an innovative program, the Learning Tree, which helped him make the transition to a special scholarship program at prestigious Hampshire College.

It wasn't easy, though. McBride felt like an outsider at first. But one of his professors helped him build his self-confidence. She told

Miami, Florida, residents protest the Department of Housing and Urban Development in 2002 for allegedly causing severe housing shortages.

him, "I honestly believe you're an amazing writer." He got one of his poems published in an anthology. He began teaching at local community colleges. In 2016, he was hired at as the director of New England Public Radio's Media Lab, an after-school program that teaches teens journalism and audio production.

her four children. Even though her old housing development felt like home, only about a third of the adults were employed. Rachel, who worked full-time, moved to a more integrated neighborhood with less joblessness.

Experiences like Rachel's stem from new policies such as the US Department of Housing and Urban Development's HOPE VI program, which aims to relocate the poor from blighted, high-density urban projects to other options. Researchers have seen some progress, including declines in the number of inner-city neighborhoods in which more than 40 percent of residents, the so-called "underclass," live below the poverty line. Participants in programs such as HOPE VI describe their new neighborhoods as less problematic but also less friendly than their old ones.

Social ties take years to build, experts say. "An effort needs to be made to connect relocated families with institutions in their new neighborhoods and to foster strong cross-status ties in mixed-income neighborhoods—either in newly redeveloped HOPE VI sites or in their new neighborhoods," wrote Susan Clampet-Lundquist, then a postdoctoral fellow at the Center for Research on Child Wellbeing at Princeton University.

Still, neighborhoods with high concentrations of poverty remain. Political economist Paul Jargowsky calls them places where the poor "not only have to cope with their own poverty but also that of those around them." Studies show that the majority of people convicted of crimes live in such heavily concentrated neighborhoods. According to the Justice Mapping Center, a Brooklyn-based research group, at one time, more than 50 percent of adult male inmates from New York City came from just fourteen districts in Manhattan, the Bronx, and Brooklyn. Eric Cadora of the Justice Mapping Center calls them "million dollar blocks" because that's what it costs the state to keep people from those areas behind bars. Instead of rehabilitating prisoners,

74   Poverty: Public Crisis or Private Struggle?

some policy experts recommend rehabilitating the neighborhoods that produce them.

Harvard University professor William Julius Wilson and other experts have noted a strong link between joblessness and criminal behavior. According to Wilson, many problems in the United States' inner-city neighborhoods—including crime, family dissolution, welfare, low levels of social organization—are related to the disappearance of work in the formal labor market. While many of the officially jobless participate in informal or illegal kinds of work such as babysitting or drug-dealing, such activities offer less financial stability than the formal workplace. Neighborhoods of high joblessness lack the kind of mainstream vitality that discourages illicit activities such as drug trafficking, crime, prostitution, and the formation of gangs.

The participation in illegal activities and the higher likelihood of being arrested as a minority in America also makes it more difficult to find a job. If a person has a felony conviction on his or her record, employers are 50 percent less likely to call him or her back after an interview or application. This creates a cycle of behavior in which people recently released from prison feel that the only way for them to make a living is to engage in illegal activities, which in turn makes them more likely to be arrested again and less able to lift themselves and their families out of poverty.

Struggling Schools

The story of Cedric Jennings, an African American student at a struggling Washington, DC, high school, is chronicled in Pulitzer Prize–winning journalist Ron Suskind's book, *A Hope in the Unseen: An American Odyssey from the Inner City to the Ivy League*. Jennings's journey from this poor urban school to Brown University shows that students in even the most troubled schools

Cedric Jennings, pictured at age twenty-two, tells his story in the book *A Hope in the Unseen*.

can succeed. However, to do so requires the kind of heroism not expected of students from more privileged schools.

Nationwide, researchers say, K–12 students are still largely divided into schools along racial lines, a trend that in urban areas can be largely attributed to housing, which in many places retain the segregated patterns of the past. A federal report from 2017 determined that 57 percent of African American students and 60 percent of Hispanic students attend schools where 75 percent of the enrollment is comprised of students of color—yet only 5 percent of white students attend such schools. In fact, the Center for American Progress reports that 40 percent of US school districts are "hypersegregated."

Many urban neighborhoods contain areas of highly concentrated poverty, meaning that a large percentage of children in these neighborhoods may suffer from poverty, too, and this can affect their performance and ability to succeed. The Center for American Progress has found that "students attending high-poverty schools … only have a 68 percent chance of graduating. In comparison, students attending low-poverty schools … have a 91 percent chance of graduating." It is more difficult to succeed at school in poor or single-parent households struggling to pay for food, much less books and school supplies.

What's worse, though, is that schools with 75–100 percent low-income African American or Hispanic populations offer fewer opportunities to excel, according to the US Government Accountability Office, which in 2016 reported that such schools "offered disproportionately fewer math, science, and college preparatory courses and had disproportionately higher rates of students who were held back in 9th grade, suspended, or expelled." Writing for the Center for American Progress, Abel McDaniels adds, "Schools that primarily serve low-income students of color often have poor curricular offerings, few extracurricular and enrichment activities, and too many inexperienced teachers." With all of these obstacles standing

The Urban Poor   77

in the way of minority and poor students, it may come as no surprise that there is a nationwide "achievement gap" between white students and students of other races—a gap that crosses socioeconomic backgrounds.

Author Jonathan Kozol criticizes these trends as a return to the old days of "separate but equal." Minority students in the inner cities, he says, feel the sting of racial isolation. A fifteen-year-old girl in Harlem told him, "It's like we're being hidden."

Education professionals seeking better opportunities for their students wrestle with a number of thorny issues. How can they attract talented teachers to inner-city schools? What kinds of tests or other measures should be used to gauge success? And, perhaps most important, how can teachers and staff build strong relationships with students?

Part of the solution seems to be increasing diversity among teachers. "Teachers of color tend to provide more culturally relevant teaching and better understand the situations that students of color may face. These factors help develop trusting teacher-student relationships," explains a 2017 Center for American Progress article. "Teachers of color tend to have more positive perceptions of students of color—both academically and behaviorally—than other teachers do. A recent study found that African American teachers are less likely than white teachers to perceive African American students' behavior as disruptive." This creates a more positive atmosphere for students of color, who feel safer and more encouraged to succeed. Yet efforts to increase the number of teachers of color have produced only modest results—an increase from 12 to 17 percent between 1987 and 2012.

After Cedric Jennings graduated from Brown University in 1999, he worked a variety of jobs and got a master's degree in social work. During his journey, he met Supreme Court Justice Clarence Thomas. The conservative African American justice warned Jennings that he could end up "caught between two worlds." Jennings returned to his hometown of Washington, DC, where he has worked as a social worker and youth minister. He coorganized a college night at his church that was well attended. The event gave him a new sense of hope that he might be able to live in one world, not two.

Today, Jennings teaches student development at Northern Virginia Community College. Part of the process of healing and growing involved reconnecting with his mother, Barbara, who died in 2013. At first, when she visited him at Brown, he was ashamed of her. "I had anxieties of people viewing her a certain way because she wasn't educated," he recalled in 2017. "I was ashamed of being ashamed of her." But despite the fact that Barbara didn't have a college diploma, and despite the day-to-day challenges she had to overcome to raise her son in a troubled urban area, Cedric found that his mother could hold her own in any conversation about college: "I didn't have to lower the bar to talk to her—in fact, I had to step up because she was a step ahead of me."

Chapter Six

THE RURAL POOR

In some parts of rural America, upward mobility is hard to come by. Those rural areas that see the most people rising out of poverty or otherwise improving their socioeconomic positions tend to be places that young adults leave when they grow up. They also tend to be places with relatively higher-quality education, with more stable families, and with more opportunities for local employment. Still, as Eleanor Krause and Richard V. Reeves observe in a 2017 Brookings Institution report, "Growing up to be better off than one's parents—upward "absolute intergenerational mobility"—looks to be far more difficult in some corners of this country than others."

Compared to urban residents, those living in rural areas tend to have lower incomes, lower life

Opposite: A trailer court houses many of the poorest residents of Lincoln, Nebraska. In 2015, it was scheduled to be razed.

expectancies, and lower education levels. They are also "more likely to be persistently poor, with at least a 20 percent poverty rate persisting for at least 30 years." Many rural areas experience a cycle of poverty that pushes locals to leave the community in search of a better life.

A Patchwork Quilt of Poverty

Dr. Edwin Smith sees poverty in the mouths of his patients.

Driving his mobile dental clinic through the hills of Appalachia, he meets people who have used Krazy Glue to reattach broken teeth. He treats patients who have pulled out their own infected teeth with pliers because they couldn't afford a dentist. And he sees the rotted and blackened teeth that are a side effect of methamphetamine drug use.

"The level of need is hard to believe unless you see it up close," Smith told the *New York Times*. Most of the people he encounters are too busy putting food on the table to worry about oral hygiene. Adults with teeth lost to sweets, tobacco, or neglect often have trouble finding work. Children frequently miss school because of the pain they suffer from dental problems. Since 2005, his nonprofit organization has treated more than forty-three thousand Kentucky children.

Such signs of poverty abound in rural America, where people often have to drive for miles to find goods and services. In a nation known for its scenic vistas of mountains and prairies, many rural residents live in terrible poverty, suffering from inadequate health care, a deficit of federal support, dwindling economic opportunities, and isolation from the rest of the nation. Settlements with fewer than 2,500 residents are considered rural. Statistics paint a bleak picture of the economic health of rural America. A majority of the nation's "persistently poor" counties are rural. In 2015, 16.7 percent of people living in rural areas were poor, compared to 13 percent of those in urban areas and 10.8 percent of the suburban population.

This may be in part because the job market in rural areas has dropped by 4.26 percent since 2008, while metropolitan employment has soared. Coal mines are shutting down. Small, local businesses such as gas stations are shutting down. There simply aren't enough jobs—or enough well-paying jobs—to sustain many of the rural poor. In rural America, job-seekers often find little more than a McDonald's or a Walmart for miles on end. These low-wage employers may be the only employers around—one reason why wages in rural areas lag behind those in urban America.

Because of its distance from major metropolitan markets, rural America rarely gets covered in the media unless there's some major tragedy. As a result, people from these areas are often stereotyped, ignored, or simply forgotten.

"Rural people are either characters out of *Deliverance* or *Mayberry R.F.D.*—outright depravity and social disintegration on one hand or overly romanticized folksiness and neo-Jeffersonian virtue on the other," wrote Mark B. Lapping in *Planning* magazine, referencing a movie and a TV show that took stereotypes of rural people to extremes. "Another stereotype is that most rural Americans are farmers," Lapping added. "In fact, with less than two percent of the entire US population engaged in agriculture, farming occupies an ever smaller niche in our rural economy."

The era of the self-sufficient family farm has long passed. These days, someone in a sparsely populated part of the country might need to drive 25 miles (40 km) to reach the nearest supermarket. For many rural Americans, a car is both a blessing and a curse. On the one hand, it opens up job opportunities. On the other hand, it sucks up money for gas and repairs.

Rural America resembles a patchwork quilt in its diversity of regions and people. Some rural areas have found a way to cash in on their scenic beauty by developing recreation and retirement opportunities, the so-called R&R industry. Others, though, lack such basic amenities as roads and telecommunications.

The Rural Poor 83

Some regions have been particularly hard-hit by poverty. The Pacific Northwest, for instance, has been dubbed the "new Appalachia" because of its loss of logging jobs. The so-called Black Belt of the Mississippi Delta lays claim to the enduring poverty of rural African Americans. In a growing swath of the country, migrant workers harvest crops and work menial jobs in meatpacking and food-processing plants. On Native American reservations in rural America, indigenous people wrestle with the highest poverty rates in the nation.

Native Americans

In the Pine Ridge Indian Reservation in South Dakota, which is governed by the Oglala Sioux Tribe and home to twenty thousand tribe members, about 80 percent of the population is unemployed. There are no banks, discount stores, libraries, or movie theaters. Oglala Lakota County, which is entirely inside the boundaries of the reservation, is the poorest county in the nation, with an average per-capita income of just $8,768, about a third of the national average. According to writer Stephanie M. Schwartz, the reservation's residents "live in abject, incomprehensible conditions rivaling, or even surpassing, that of many Third World countries."

According to official estimates, more than 53 percent of the population lives below the poverty level, though other analyses place it above 80 percent. Low levels of health and education have decimated the community. More than seven in ten students drop out of school. About 85 percent of Lakota families suffer the effects of alcoholism. Infant mortality is three times the national rate, tuberculosis eight times the national rate, and the life expectancy is just 66.81 years, lower than anywhere else in the United States. Many homes lack basic water and sewage systems as well as electricity.

On the Pine Ridge Indian Reservation in South Dakota, children play in front of a house provided by the Tribal Housing Authority.

The Sioux are not alone in their plight. One in four Alaska Natives and Native Americans lives below the poverty line, twice the national average.

Nevertheless, tribal leaders have not given up hope. The Sioux at Pine Ridge have developed innovative proposals for new culture and language programs, business development, substance abuse treatment, and alternative education initiatives. They sought to revoke the liquor licenses of stores in nearby Whiteclay, Nebraska, where many on the reservation were buying their alcohol. However, the reservation now faces new challenges in light of budget cuts proposed by the Trump administration. A proposed 25 percent budget cut to the food stamp program would affect approximately half of Pine Ridge residents. A proposed 15 percent cut of the Interior Department's budget would impact the Bureau of Indian Affairs and nearly two million Native Americans.

While the Sioux oppose gambling on religious grounds, other tribes have established casinos to lift their people out of poverty. The results have been mixed. Some casinos have brought not only great wealth but also a new set of problems.

The Rural Poor

Consider the case of Foxwoods Casino in the southeastern corner of Connecticut. Established on the site of an old Pequot tribe reservation, the casino brought the Pequot back from the brink of extinction. In the early 1970s, only Elizabeth George and her sister remained in a dilapidated house on the Pequot reservation, which lacked electricity, roads, and businesses. When the state threatened to turn the ancestral land into a park, the elderly George pleaded with her relatives to return to the reservation.

Soon after George died in 1973, her grandson, Richard "Skip" Hayward, moved onto the site. Hayward, a pipe-fitter and welder, wrote to faraway relatives, urging them to join him, and some did. It was touch-and-go at first, but the group's luck changed for the better once they opened a high-stakes bingo parlor in 1986. Two years later, the federal government passed the Indian Gaming Regulatory Act, allowing the tribe to expand its bingo hall into a casino.

People began contacting the tribe, claiming to be Pequot. If individuals could trace their family lineage back to a Pequot listed in a 1900 or 1910 census, they could claim membership in the tribe. Membership and revenue swelled. Limos snaked through the town. Within five years of its opening, the glitzy attraction grossed over $1 billion annually. Mansions and luxury cars dotted the new gated community. Under the tribe's profit-sharing plan, each member aged eighteen and older, working or not, would receive about $100,000 a year.

However, with unprecedented wealth and power came new challenges. Many young people felt no need to work or go to school. Some took drugs. Internal dissension rocked the tribe. Racial tensions flared. Dissatisfaction with Hayward's leadership grew. In 1998, he lost his bid to retain the chairmanship.

Of about 560 federally recognized tribes, approximately 244 have established gambling operations. Of these, only a fraction has generated substantial wealth for their members. Many casinos are located in areas too remote to be profitable.

Migrant Workers

Norma Flores stood under the scorching sun, drenched in sweat, with an acre or more of weeds to hoe. It was a typical July day for Flores, a teenager who worked alongside her parents in the fields twelve hours a day, seven days a week, every summer. She had a sunburn, aches, and rashes to show for her hard work.

In April 2009, a federal judge refused to close the mobile-home encampment where migrant worker Victoriano Lemus lived with his son.

"As you stand in the middle of the field and look around you, your mind is swarmed with millions of reasons why to pursue a college education," Flores, then eighteen years old, wrote in an essay for Motivation Education & Training, Inc., a nonprofit organization that serves farmworkers. "Being a migrant also served as an opportunity to see what a sacrifice my parents have gone through to give us the opportunity to achieve all our dreams."

Migrant workers like Flores make up a group of Americans some experts call "the poorest of the poor." Children who work on farms are governed by different laws than those in any other occupation. While the minimum employment age for nonagricultural work is fourteen, young farm laborers can start at age twelve if accompanied by a parent. Youths who are fourteen or older can work unlimited hours in the fields before or after school hours. Those in other occupations are permitted to work only three hours per day while school is in session.

Many young people in migrant families start the school year late and end early so they can work the spring, summer, and fall crops. To stay at grade level, they often cram in extra homework before they leave or mail it in to their hometown schools. Nevertheless, participants in programs for migrant workers also describe a positive side to the work. Families working in the fields develop a special kind of closeness during their long days together.

Farmworkers toil in blistering heat and drenching rains. Many suffer injuries and poor health from exposure to pesticides. Painful welts and sore bodies from heavy picking bags are common. Some unscrupulous bosses berate workers and push them to work harder and faster than reasonably possible. If laborers complain about their conditions or try to organize, employers might threaten to fire or deport them.

The workers have reason to be afraid. During the administration of President George W. Bush, the Department of Labor sided more with employers and failed to enforce labor laws. In particular, the Bush administration's order to increase checks into whether workers had Social Security numbers created a wave of fear among those undocumented immigrants who had invented a string of digits or used identification that belonged to someone else.

Immigrants who protest working conditions run the risk of being fired. Many therefore work long hours for lower wages than could be legally paid to a documented worker or American citizen.

Past Mistakes and Future Hopes

By her own admission, Gwen Boggs had "messed up." At the age of fifteen, she began running with a bad crowd in her hometown, a small mining outpost in Appalachia. She stayed up all hours, drinking and smoking marijuana, dropped out of high school, and got pregnant. After marrying and working in a variety of fast-food restaurants, Gwen decided she wanted a better life for her children.

Sociologist Cynthia M. Duncan profiled Gwen Boggs along with two other women—Caroline Gage and Deborah Shannon—in similar circumstances in her book, *Worlds Apart: Why Poverty Persists in Rural America*. Based on the author's extensive interviews, these three composite figures showed the role communities play in helping or hurting individuals who want a second chance in life.

Like Gwen, Caroline Gage longed to correct the mistakes of the past. One of thirteen children in a poor Mississippi Delta family afflicted by domestic violence, she missed so much school because of her family responsibilities that the principal told her to stop coming after eighth grade. To escape a life of drudgery in the fields, she married at the age of fifteen, but soon found her husband was abusive, so she moved back to her hometown.

The Rural Poor 89

"A Little Meth and a Lot of Booze"

In the American West, big skies, green pastures, and majestic mountains stretch on for miles. Yet against this seemingly idyllic backdrop, an unusually high percentage of young people are drinking to excess, vomiting, passing out, and sometimes dying in alcohol-related car crashes.

Why is there so much heavy drinking in rural America? Insiders point to one main reason: boredom. With little to do outside of organized sports, many young people gather together to get intoxicated. Drugs, too, have made their way into small towns. The use of OxyContin, a prescription synthetic pain reliever, has infiltrated rural areas. So, too, has methamphetamine, a highly addictive drug manufactured from readily available ingredients in rural labs. Murders and other serious crimes have rocked small towns swept up in the drug trade.

The Muskie School of Public Service at the University of Southern Maine describes substance abuse among rural youth as "A Little Meth and a Lot of Booze." In another study involving an anonymous survey of rural Mississippi middle school students, a shocking 17 percent of students had driven after drinking alcohol and just under half—45 percent—had ridden with a driver who had been drinking. Because so many rural children drive tractors and ATVs at an early age, they're apt to combine drinking with driving even though they're too young to have a license.

Statistics tell a sobering tale about rural substance abuse: young adults (eighteen to twenty-five) in the smallest rural areas use methamphetamine and OxyContin at twice the rate of their urban counterparts. Children (twelve to seventeen) from the smallest rural areas are more likely to have used alcohol, engaged in binge drinking, and driven under the influence than urban children.

Substance abuse is a big problem in rural America, even among teenagers. But finding treatment can be especially hard in these areas.

Getting treatment in rural areas can be a challenge. Treatment centers can be few and far between, with little public transportation to get to them. Available facilities often lack the expertise of metropolitan health centers. Also, the culture of rural America emphasizes individualism and self-sufficiency, making it difficult for some people to seek help.

The Rural Poor

She had five children and went to work in a sewing factory. Caroline wanted to move to her uncle's farm in Arkansas but didn't have the money.

Deborah Shannon also grew up in a troubled family. The daughter of an alcoholic father who abused her mother, Deborah dropped out of school and ran wild in her old mill town in northern New England. After having a child, she received welfare as a single mother for four years, then found part-time work in a restaurant, married an old friend, and thought about developing a career.

Of the three women trying to rise out of poverty, Deborah alone succeeded. In Gwen's town in Appalachia and Caroline's in the Mississippi Delta, middle-class residents often side with the wealthy coal barons and plantation bosses to keep the poor isolated in separate schools and menial part-time jobs. In Deborah's community in northern New England, on the other hand, everyone "rubs elbows" with everyone else.

Whereas Gwen's and Caroline's tattered clothes and manner of speaking set them apart from the mainstream, Deborah blended in. Even though Deborah grew up in a troubled, chaotic family, she developed relationships in school and in the community that gave her a sort of "cultural tool kit" to turn her life around. She got a good education and mixed easily with children from the middle class. The communities where Gwen and Caroline lived, on the other hand, gave them few tools for upward mobility.

Deborah eventually married an old classmate from a solid blue-collar family and took steps toward becoming a nurse. Gwen, on the other hand, put her dreams of a teaching career on hold because she lacked the resources and encouragement to go back to school. Similarly, Caroline held out little hope of ever leaving the Mississippi Delta.

Duncan, the author of *Worlds Apart*, found education to be linked to race and class. In the highly stratified communities, the wealthy sent their children to separate, often private, schools and vetoed tax increases to pay for improvements in public education. Administrators who rose to their positions through political patronage let school buildings deteriorate and failed to bring in state and federal resources for education programs.

In the Mississippi Delta, for instance, whites had little social contact with African Americans. Whites enjoyed economic power and security while most African Americans like Caroline were poor and powerless. Patterns established during slavery persisted long after emancipation; for instance, around two-thirds of whites had a high school degree or more, compared to only one-third of African Americans. Nearly one-fifth of whites had completed college, compared to only about 4 percent of African Americans.

"The path out of poverty is remarkably similar across all three communities described here," wrote Duncan. "In every case, a good education is the key that unlocks and expands the cultural tool kits of the have-nots, and thus gives them the potential to bring about lasting social change in their persistently poor communities."

Without the necessary resources and tools, upward economic mobility is all the more difficult—and to those left behind, it may feel next to impossible.

Chapter Seven

HOMELESSNESS AND THE WORK FORCE

Many of the nation's poorest people live without the most basic necessities. They not only go without food, but many find themselves without shelter, living on the streets and trying to survive inclement weather, dangerous encounters, and constant pressure to leave communities where they aren't welcome. Because many of the homeless don't have access to bathing facilities or nice clothes, it is all the more difficult for them to find jobs that can put them on the path to greater financial security. Social factors such as toxic family situations and mental health problems drive many to live on the streets, but economic factors such as high unemployment and high cost of living also cause homelessness. As a result, half a million people find themselves homeless in the United States on any given night.

Opposite: At a homeless encampment near downtown Detroit, Michigan, Charles "C. J." Jones keeps a fire going.

Homelessness in the United States

Rusty Booker wanted to run away from his alcoholic mother and abusive stepfather—but he didn't know where to go. Although he had been in foster care for a brief time, the state had returned him to his mother and stepfather. Rusty called his former foster parents, who told him about the national Safe Place program. He made his way to the public library with the Safe Place sign out front. From there, he went to a YMCA shelter in Louisville, Kentucky.

"I felt safe for the first time in many years," he recalled.

Seventeen-year-old Rusty told his story to members of Congress holding hearings on one of the nation's most vulnerable populations: homeless youth. People younger than twenty-four comprise more than 30 percent of the homeless population, but they are one of many groups of people who lack shelter in the United States every day.

Causes of Homelessness

In addition to runaways, missing children, and young people thrown out of their homes, the homeless in America include large populations of the mentally ill, substance abusers, victims of domestic violence, minorities, and families unable to find affordable housing.

Whatever their circumstances, homeless individuals typically suffer from feelings of shame and embarrassment. They experience rates of depression almost twice as high as the general population.

Deinstitutionalization—the process of moving severely mentally ill people out of large state institutions—aimed to provide a more humane and less restrictive form of treatment. The movement began in 1955 with the widespread introduction of chlorpromazine, commonly known as Thorazine, an antipsychotic medication. Since then, more than 90 percent of state psychiatric hospital beds have been eliminated.

Although some discharged patients have successfully made the transition to living on their own in the community, many others floundered and stopped taking their medication. Civil libertarians have opposed forced hospitalization except in cases where the mentally ill pose a clear danger to themselves or others. With few psychiatric beds left, many of the mentally ill have ended up in general hospitals, nursing homes, prisons, homeless shelters, and on the streets. While about 7.5 percent of adults in the United States suffered from a severe mental illness in 2016, individuals with severe mental illness comprise 20–25 percent of the homeless population, according to the National Institute of Mental Health. The Treatment Advocacy Center reports that in some places, this can be even higher, ranging from 33–50 percent of chronically homeless people.

About one in five homeless people is experiencing a chronic substance abuse disorder. That is, they use alcohol and drugs extensively, and this use either led to their homelessness, or has been exacerbated by their time on the street. Some homeless people turn to substance abuse as a form of self-medication, or out of hopelessness for a way out of their situation.

A disproportionate number of homeless youth identify as lesbian, gay, bisexual, and transgender (LGBT)—as many as 40 percent of all homeless young people. "Unfortunately, a good deal of information suggests that LGBT youth experience higher rates of homelessness precisely because of their sexual orientation or gender identity," the Center for American Progress reported in 2013. "Youth are coming out to their families at younger ages, and all too often are being met with family rejection or abusive responses that force them out of their homes." While homeless,

Homelessness and the Work Force   97

this same group is also at higher risk for sexual exploitation, drug abuse, and physical assault.

Even veterans are at risk for homelessness. According to the Substance Abuse and Mental Health Services Administration, "The demanding environments of military life and experiences of combat, during which many veterans experience psychological distress, can be further complicated by substance use and related disorders." With more than 18 percent of veterans from the wars in Iraq and Afghanistan experiencing depression or post-traumatic stress disorder (PTSD), rates of suicide, mental health conditions, and trauma are high among this group, putting them at greater risk for homelessness. More than thirty-nine thousand veterans faced homelessness on any given night in 2016.

There is good news when it comes to homelessness, however. Between 2007 and 2017, overall homelessness in the United States decreased 14 percent, and those experiencing chronic homelessness decreased 18 percent between 2010 and 2017, according to the US Department of Housing and Urban Development (HUD). This success has been attributed in part to efforts by the US Department of Veterans Affairs and to Opening Doors, a program launched in 2010 that helps people at risk of losing their housing and provides quick access to crisis help and shelters. Still, places such as California and New York City continue to see large numbers of people living on the streets due to the lack of affordable housing.

Rusty's path from homelessness to college-bound high school student was a bumpy one. He abused drugs and alcohol, fought with foster parents, and landed in jail. Finally, he returned to his first caseworker, who helped put him on the road to success.

Who Is Experiencing Homelessness?

Researchers divide the homeless into three groups: the sheltered, the unsheltered, and the doubled-up. While about two-thirds of the homeless live in shelters or transitional housing, about one-third live or camp outdoors, in abandoned buildings, or in their cars. The doubled-up are people living with family or friends on a temporary basis.

HUD reports the racial and ethnic composition of the homeless to be 47 percent white, 41 percent African American, 7 percent multiracial, 3 percent Native American, 1.5 percent Pacific Islander, and 1.2 percent Asian. Nearly 22 percent were Latino or Hispanic. Based on these figures, minorities in the United States are more likely to experience homelessness than whites.

About 16 percent of homeless people are chronically homeless—that is, they have a disability and have been homeless for a continuous period of at least one year, or have been homeless at least four times in three years.

David and Gina Christian and their four children ended up in transitional housing in Dallas, Texas, after David lost his job fixing cars. Gina was a temporary worker at a nursing home and didn't make enough money to cover the family's expenses. Like Gina, many people unable to find permanent positions take temporary jobs that often fail to provide regular wages and benefits. Before getting help from the Interfaith House in Dallas, David sold tires from their two cars to pay for their nightly meals of beans and rice. In an interview with *Time* magazine, Gina said, "I felt degraded, like I was less than human."

Criminalizing the Homeless

One cold night in February, Augustine Betancourt tucked himself into his cardboard box and fell asleep on a bench in a small park in New York City. At about 1:30 a.m., two police officers awakened him. It was his first arrest.

For Betancourt, a thirty-three-year-old army veteran who had spiraled into homelessness after his odd jobs tapered off, sleeping on the street had become a way of life. With the help

"Criminal" Begging?

Is begging protected by the First Amendment? That's the question the courts faced after police in New York City arrested Jennifer Loper for loitering in 1992. Loper had moved out of her parents' suburban home to beg on the streets of New York. In Loper's case, the courts agreed that her right to free speech had been violated because the sidewalks historically served as a public forum. However, in cases of "aggressive panhandling," officials often take a harder line.

Numerous municipalities have passed regulations against aggressive panhandling to prohibit activities such as following passersby after they have refused to give money or intimidating people into giving. In Gretna, Virginia, town leaders passed an emergency ordinance banning aggressive panhandling after residents were awakened at night by beggars banging on their doors. Town Manager David Lilly told *USA Today*, "It's being fueled by the crack industry."

Many experts recommend that conflicts over panhandling be resolved informally rather than taken to court. For instance, municipal leaders might adopt public education campaigns to encourage people to give to charities instead of panhandlers. Some merchants offer panhandlers odd jobs so they won't need to beg outside their stores. And, instead of arresting panhandlers, police officers typically tell them to "move along." Indeed, some officers cultivate panhandlers as informants because they know what is happening in the streets.

Such incidents of "criminalizing the homeless" highlight the difficult questions local officials face when conflicts about public space pit the civil liberties of the unhoused against the rights of the majority. Do residents and merchants who object to homeless individuals urinating and defecating in public have legitimate grounds for police action? How

In subzero temperatures on a Chicago, Illinois, bridge, a homeless man begs for change.

should communities deal with dangers to the public such as tripping over people and objects on the sidewalks, intimidation of passersby caused by aggressive begging, and public discomfort caused by poor personal hygiene? What is the best way to balance compassion for the homeless with the public's right to clean and safe streets?

of a lawyer he found in a soup kitchen, he filed a class-action lawsuit against the city for violating his civil rights.

"After you spend a certain amount of time in the streets, as difficult as your circumstances are, they become a routine," Betancourt said in an interview. "You want to avoid disruption of the familiar—even if it's sleeping in an alley."

Although Betancourt lost his nine-year legal battle with the city, he ultimately achieved a measure of victory. His lawyer persuaded him to move into a single-room-occupancy hotel. Betancourt finally sought treatment for his illnesses—major depression and an array of personality and anxiety disorders, including social phobias—that had been undiagnosed for years.

Cases like Betancourt's have found their way to courts throughout the nation, with mixed results. In Los Angeles, for instance, the homeless won a victory by being allowed to sleep on sidewalks as long as they didn't block building entrances. On the other hand, municipal officials in Orlando, Florida, passed an "anti-feeding ordinance" to crack down on churches and activists who had been feeding large groups of homeless people in downtown parks.

Advocates for the homeless argue that the money used to prosecute the homeless could be better spent on programs to help them. In some cities, police sweeps are giving way to outreach work by officers and service providers. Also, policymakers nationwide are working to get the homeless out of temporary shelters and into permanent housing.

Housing the Homeless

Nancy Quinn dragged an old box spring from the garbage to her makeshift home under an overpass in the South Bronx. Huddled under six blankets, she spoke to a reporter for *New York* magazine about her life as a drug addict, sexual-abuse victim, and prostitute.

Jane Footer prepares for bed at a homeless shelter in Portland, Maine.

"I have no pimp," she told the reporter. "You want to hear something bad? You want to know who my pimp is? My stem is my pimp. My crack pipe."

A thirty-eight-year-old mother of three, Quinn avoided homeless shelters because they typically required people to stop using drugs or at least to enter a rehabilitation program or get counseling. Several years had passed since Augustine Betancourt was arrested for sleeping in a cardboard box. As mayors had changed in New York City, so, too, had policy regarding the homeless.

New research had shown that giving homes to the homeless could actually save money by reducing the costs spent on emergency rooms, shelter beds, jail cells, psychiatric hospitals, and other services. Experts, though, say that living alone can be a challenge, especially for individuals struggling with physical and mental health issues. Support services are crucial, but even then, not everyone accepts the help. As Quinn's story shows, helping the homeless build better lives is no simple matter.

In 2008, outreach workers in New York convinced Quinn to accept a free room in an apartment house about a half-mile from the overpass where she once lived. Reconnecting with her teenage son had shown her how far she had fallen. At first, Quinn reveled in her new home, delighting in the shower and the electricity. But one night, she slipped out to smoke crack. She was arrested and charged with a Class-A misdemeanor, her thirty-ninth arrest. Once she was released, she returned to her home below the overpass, not the apartment.

She didn't want to smoke in the apartment, but she wasn't ready to get clean either. Instead, she wanted to have it both ways: to have a new life but not to give up her old life.

"I want to get nice and high," she told the reporter. "I need something to eat, and then I can go there and lie down."

Welfare Reform

Michelle Gordon bounced from job to job. A single mother with four children, she worked as a call-center employee, a nurse's aide, and a janitorial supervisor, but nothing took. She moved back in with her mother and mowed lawns to make ends meet. Michelle described her life since welfare reform as "a little bit of a roller coaster."

Mary Bradford, on the other hand, made a successful transition from welfare to work. Also a single mother, she landed a clerical job that led to a supervisory position in the same company. In a matter of ten years, she doubled her earnings.

These two women, profiled in *USA Today*, illustrate both the successes and the frustrations of welfare reform. Passed in 1996, the Personal Responsibility and Work Opportunity Reconciliation Act aimed to end welfare dependence by promoting education, job training, family responsibility, and work. The act requires recipients, who are mostly single mothers, to work at least part-time after receiving assistance for two years. It puts a five-year lifetime limit on benefits.

Using a carrot-and-stick approach, the Temporary Assistance for Needy Families program offers recipients help with childcare, job training, and transportation if they work—and sanctions if they don't. States can make exceptions for certain hard-to-employ individuals. The 2006 renewal of the welfare act tightened work requirements.

Welfare reform has dramatically reduced welfare caseloads. The number of welfare recipients dropped from 12.2 million in August 1996 to 4.5 million in June 2005, a 64 percent decline. Critics of welfare reform, however, argue that many former recipients end up in low-wage jobs with inadequate childcare and health coverage.

Clearly, some individuals in welfare-to-work programs do better than others. Those coming from impoverished neighborhoods where few people hold steady jobs face special challenges, especially if their support systems break down.

Consider the case of Carolyn (not her real name). A single mother featured in Sharon Hays' book *Flat Broke with Children: Women in the Age of Welfare Reform*, Carolyn had left her husband after he abused her. The effects of the abuse led to a nervous breakdown requiring hospitalization. Carolyn lost her job and went on welfare.

When her daughter was two, Carolyn returned to work. Three years later, her sister was imprisoned for selling drugs. Carolyn took in her three nieces (ages three, nine, and twelve) so they wouldn't end up in foster care. She got a second job to bring in more money and juggled her many responsibilities with the help of her brother and sister-in-law, who assisted with childcare and transportation. But when they moved out of town, they left Carolyn dependent on public transportation and paid caregivers. Next, she got laid off from one of her jobs. The stress of her situation began to affect her health, resulting in serious heart problems. Her doctor urged her to "take it easy."

Carolyn returned to her local welfare office. Would she be able to find a program to help her back on her feet? Her future hung in the balance, dependent on the public programs in her geographical area. No matter how hard she tried, she needed help—and in that, she wasn't alone.

Trial and Error

Fred Keller, the head of Cascade Engineering, Inc., in Grand Rapids, Michigan, wanted to help people make the leap from welfare to work. Not only did Keller believe such a move would benefit society, he also thought it could be good business. In addition to the financial incentives the state offered to participate in its welfare-to-work program, Cascade would get a boost in productivity if it could retain a new corps of dedicated workers. However, Keller found hiring people from impoverished circumstances much more of a challenge than he had originally expected.

A case study in the Stanford Social Innovation Review describes how Cascade's early attempts at hiring welfare-to-work employees failed. During the company's first try, former welfare recipients used a company van to get alcohol and drugs. Next, the company tried partnering with Burger King, offering prospective employees a chance to advance from the fast-food industry to plastics after six months. However, none of the workers stayed at Burger King long enough to make it to Cascade.

Learning from these two failures, Keller decided to try again. This time, everyone at Cascade attended a "Hidden Rules" training based on Dr. Ruby Payne's book, *A Framework for Understanding Poverty*. In her book, Payne describes how people live by the rules of their own social class—poor, middle class, or wealthy—which are usually unfamiliar to outsiders.

Keller brought in social workers to work at Cascade. The company had learned from past failures that employees needed more support than they could get from off-site caseworkers

Alyson Howard was one of forty participants in a welfare-to-work program in Pittsburgh, Pennsylvania, in 2006. She is pictured working at Goodwill Industries, a partner in the program.

with high caseloads. The new staffers helped employees deal with everything from broken-down cars to domestic violence. Instead of punishing a battered employee for being unable to work, Cascade's team would tell him or her to take the week off, after which time the worker would return to work grateful for the support. The company had learned that by making employees feel important and valued, it could boost productivity.

"The organization actually is more energized," Keller said. "People are more focused because they know that the organization values everyone there and we actually get more done." Since 1999, Cascade's program has helped eight hundred people start a new career and a new life.

Better Jobs and Better Wages

Jeffrey Evans lost his $14.55-an-hour factory job after the plant shut down in the wake of a labor dispute. He searched for a new job but found nothing comparable to his old one. Settling for sporadic construction work, he saw his income cut in half. Forty-nine-year-old Evans had to move back with his mother, Shirley Sheline, seventy-three, who had worked at the same auto parts plant.

"Can you believe it, a grown man forced to move back with his mother?" Sheline asked a reporter for the *New York Times*.

Stories such as Evans's have become increasingly common as high-paying manufacturing jobs give way to lower-paying positions in the service sector. Some of the job loss in the manufacturing sector can be blamed on factories moving their plants overseas to take advantage of cheaper labor as a result of free-trade agreements such as the North American Free Trade Agreement (NAFTA). At the same time, more employers throughout the United States have scaled back benefits and made jobs part-time, temporary, or freelance.

Labor unions have long helped workers gain better pay and working conditions from their employers. However, the George W. Bush administration curbed the power of unions by weakening enforcement of labor laws. In 2008, after reviewing a sampling of cases brought to the Wage and Hour Division of the Labor Department, the nonpartisan Government Accountability Office reported that the division had failed to adequately investigate complaints that workers were not paid the minimum wage, were denied mandatory overtime, or were not paid their last paychecks.

Is a low-wage future inevitable? Not necessarily, wrote Beth Shulman, the author of *The Betrayal of Work: How Low-Wage Jobs Fail 30 Million Americans*. Shulman argued that nothing about the jobs themselves makes work in manufacturing "good" and positions in the service sector "bad." As she saw it, the good jobs of tomorrow could be in the service sector. These jobs are growing, and many can't be outsourced. While workers in India might be able to give you technical assistance for your computer over the phone, they're not physically close enough to pour your coffee at the local diner. Whether or not the service jobs of the future can provide the same kind of decent pay as yesterday's manufacturing jobs remains to be seen.

"A critical fact is that there is nothing inherent in putting together cars or handling molten steel that makes these jobs 'good.'

Teamsters in Los Angeles, California, speak out in favor of labor unions on International Workers' Day on May 1, 2018.

In fact, at one time these jobs were hazardous, low-wage jobs that provided few benefits," Shulman explained. In exactly the same way, nothing is inherently "bad" about the job of a childcare worker, nursing-home aide, security guard, emergency medical technician, janitor, or hotel worker. Shulman concluded that it is time we discarded the notion that something in a particular job chains it forever to low pay and miserable conditions.

Shulman offered a three-step solution for boosting the pay of low-wage jobs. First, raise the minimum wage. Second, reward good employers. Third, pave the way for workers to unionize. Antilabor campaigns by employers have forced many workers into submission. She recommended stiffer penalties for employers who harass, intimidate, or fire workers for their union activities and that these employers be prohibited from receiving public monies. In addition, she called for new mechanisms to prevent employers from stalling to prevent a contract.

A Living Wage

Jamila Mozeb, a twenty-six-year-old single mother of four, couldn't afford to take a day off from work to file for government assistance. Her $9.50-an-hour job left her having to "rotate" her bills, making partial or late payments. To keep food costs low, she sometimes cooked a big pot of spaghetti and made it last for a week.

However, in the spring of 2007, Mozeb got a new burst of hope. Maryland had passed the nation's first statewide living-wage ordinance, following in the footsteps of the many municipalities that had implemented such standards. Maryland's law, which took effect in the fall of 2007, boosted Mozeb's hourly wage to $11.30 an hour. The required minimum pay has increased as the cost of living has, and as of September 2017, the minimum is $13.79 per hour in more expensive areas to live and $10.36 per hour in the rest of the state.

Mozeb is one of the beneficiaries of more than 130 living-wage ordinances that have won approval across America since Baltimore passed the first such bill in 1994. In addition, twenty-nine states and Washington, DC, have increased their minimum-wage levels above the federal minimum. A living wage tends to be higher than a minimum wage because it takes into account the real costs of living in a particular geographical area.

Living-wage ordinances vary in their scale and scope. Some are limited to government contractors working on municipal projects. Others extend to all employers in a particular jurisdiction.

Critics of living-wage ordinances argue that they jeopardize employment by prompting employers to leave town rather than pay workers higher wages. However, some community leaders say they'd rather not have such employers anyway.

In particular, big-box retailers such as Walmart have come under fire for putting small competitors out of business, turning possible green spaces into vast parking lots, and failing to provide employees with decent wages and benefits. As David Barron, a professor at Harvard Law School, put it: "This surge of interest in regulating big-box retail shows that, at last, American cities are beginning to think of themselves as choosers rather than beggars."

The Unemployment Rate

As a result of the Great Recession, the unemployment rate in the United States took a dive, reaching 10 percent in 2009. Those who are considered "unemployed" are people actively looking for work and available to work who, nonetheless, cannot find a job. Consumer spending declined dramatically as people struggled to reduce their debt and boost their savings accounts. In part because more that 85 million jobs relied upon consumer spending, the economy lost nearly 8.7 million jobs. "Consumer behavior has both reflected and contributed to the slow pace of recovery," said Ben Bernanke, chairman of the Federal Reserve, in 2011.

As more people struggled to make ends meet, homelessness increased 3 percent—by roughly twenty thousand people—between 2008 and 2009. The number of homeless families also saw an increase of 4 percent.

As of March 2018, the unemployment rate was 4.1 percent—a seventeen-year low. The poverty rate had decreased dramatically since the Great Recession. For this reason, it is easy to see why the unemployment rate is directly tied to Americans' ability to rise out or stay out of poverty.

Chapter Eight

IN SEARCH OF SOLUTIONS

The battle against poverty is ongoing as new challenges and circumstances arise. Different groups of people face different obstacles to financial stability depending on where they live, their race or ethnicity, their country of origin, their age, and other factors. Economic downturns can wreak havoc on the unemployment rate and create more poverty and homelessness. Eliminating poverty completely seems to some an impossible task—but much can be done to improve Americans' ability to achieve financial security.

A Game of Musical Chairs

Poverty has dogged America for centuries. From poorhouses to welfare reform, people have long felt the pinch of not having enough. The United States is one of the richest nations on earth, yet one in eight Americans still lives below the poverty level.

Opposite: Residents of a tent city for the homeless in Sacramento, California, are pictured in April 2009.

Some progress has been made over the years. The poverty rate among the elderly has declined dramatically as a result of Social Security. Reductions in teenage pregnancy and increases in the number of single parents in the workforce have also brought promising results.

However, experts argue that more can be done. In his book, *One Nation, Underprivileged*, author Mark Robert Rank describes poverty in the United States in terms of two well-known games: Monopoly and Musical Chairs.

First, imagine a game of Monopoly in which the players start out with different amounts of cash and property. This, Rank writes, is like social class in America, which tends to be passed down from generation to generation. Those in the upper echelons have an advantage over everyone else.

Next, Rank likens success in the United States to a game of Musical Chairs. Without enough decent-paying jobs to go around, not everyone gets a seat at the table of plenty. A majority of Americans have experienced poverty at some point in their adult lives, according to Rank.

As Rank and other experts see it, the nation can harness its long-standing values of work, opportunity, family, and thrift to help build a brighter future for all Americans. The personal responsibility advocated by conservatives and the social safety net championed by liberals need to go hand-in-hand, they say. Because poverty affects all aspects of life, experts recommend a comprehensive approach that links services. Here are some examples of innovative measures that have improved the lives of real people.

New Jobs and Hard Work

During the Great Depression, President Franklin D. Roosevelt's New Deal created millions of jobs in public works. Plans for economic growth in the twenty-first century call for a similar marriage of job creation with infrastructure upgrades. Public investment in roads, bridges, schools, and public buildings could substantially boost employment.

Some other steps that have been taken or suggested to improve jobs and wages include providing income-loss insurance for individuals who lose their jobs and take lower-paying work; offering wage subsidies to employers to stimulate job creation; developing public-service employment programs; creating new green-collar jobs for the environment; distributing pay more equitably to reduce the gap between high- and low-wage earners; and making transportation to work more affordable and convenient.

Creating more jobs isn't enough, though; many argue that rewarding hard work is also important, and this is achieved in part through the tax code. Sandra Rascon, a health aide and single mother of four, got good news from her tax preparer: she was eligible for a huge tax credit. By filing for the Earned Income Tax Credit (EITC), she'd receive a refund worth nearly two months of her salary.

"You can use the refund for anything. But I was on a strict budget to buy this home," she told the *Los Angeles Times*. "It was my dream. I can't believe I was able to do it. This year, I'm going to use the refund to buy furniture."

The Earned Income Tax Credit has the same effect as a pay raise, although the costs are shouldered by the government rather than the employer. For a head of household earning $7.50 an hour, the EITC effectively raises the hourly wage several dollars.

However, Rascon, like many workers, missed out on thousands of dollars for years because she didn't know she was eligible. Enacted in 1975, the EITC was significantly expanded in the 1990s. Most benefits go to families with children, but some researchers recommend expanding the EITC to provide for individuals without children.

Access to Good Health Coverage

When Tamar Guerra made the transition from welfare to work, she lost her Medicaid benefits. She missed the security of being able to go to her old HMO (a health maintenance organization that provides a range of services to members) whenever she or one of her sons got sick.

"If you have a pain in your finger, they send you to a specialist for your finger," she said in *The Missing Class* by Katherine S. Newman and Victor Tan Chen. "They really take care of you until they make sure you receive appropriate attention."

Eventually, Guerra learned about her eligibility for health insurance through the state of New York. She was eager to enroll. However, to apply, she would need to take a day off from her new job in a cosmetics factory, something she was not ready to do because she worried she'd lose her job.

Guerra's experiences are common. A strong connection exists between poverty and poor health for a number of reasons, including high stress, poor nutrition, unhealthy environments, and the high cost of health care.

Nationwide, the state Child Health Insurance Program (CHIP) implemented in 1998 has helped expand health-care coverage for children, but many families do not know how to (or know that they can) enroll for the benefits. Streamlining and simplifying the application process could improve access.

The Patient Protection and Affordable Care Act of 2010 required that all Americans have some form of health insurance. Since its enactment, more Americans than ever are covered, either through their employer or through federal or state exchanges where they can purchase health coverage directly from an insurer. The country's lowest-income individuals and families are eligible to be covered by Medicaid at no cost. However, many have raised concerns over the increasing premiums of these plans, and some have preferred to pay the penalty for not being insured rather than to pay the steep monthly costs of coverage.

The Affordable Care Act remains under attack by conservatives, who want to repeal or replace the law, and some provisions have been repealed. The United States has not yet achieved a highly effective universal health coverage system—and some argue that requiring universal coverage is not the most effective solution.

Affordable Housing

Cartina M., a twenty-seven-year-old single parent and department-store clerk whose last name was withheld, was living in a high-crime neighborhood in Chicago when she learned of her eligibility for a housing voucher program. The voucher enabled her to move to a condominium in Oak Park, a desirable suburb, and cut her commute by one-and-a-half hours a day, according to HUD. However, not everyone is so fortunate. Many apartment-seekers cannot find landlords willing to accept their vouchers. Nor can they afford to purchase their own homes.

Still, many have benefited from this program. A 1986 tax credit designed to encourage investment in affordable housing has led to the construction of three million low-income apartments. The $9-billion-a-year program has benefitted many like Cartina who are seeking safer neighborhoods and assistance to avoid homelessness. However, the Republican tax plan approved in December 2017 reduced the value of credits for building affordable housing, and experts expect that the growth and construction of subsidized housing will decrease by 235,000 units over the next ten years.

"It's the greatest shock to the affordable-housing system since the Great Recession," said Michael Novogradac, managing partner of a San Francisco–based accounting firm.

Improving Childcare and Education

Jeremy Walton, a preschool teacher in Milwaukee, Wisconsin, understands the importance of developing young minds. "The way I look at it," Walton told the local *Journal-Sentinel,* "they are the people that are going to be writing my prescriptions. They're going to be teaching my grandchildren. They're going to be protecting my home. They're going to be lawyers and dentists."

Walton was teaching in one of the twenty-six states that, a decade ago, had increased funding for prekindergarten. In 2016–2017, thirty states invested even more money in pre-K programs, and nationwide, there had been a 47 percent increase in funding for such programs in the previous five years. Just six states were not providing such funds. Researchers cite quality early-childhood education as a key ingredient in educational success and in moving people out of poverty.

Quality education in early childhood has been shown to help people rise out of poverty.

First, experts suggest a more generous system of child-care benefits such as those seen in European countries. Second, they recommend a number of steps to improve public schools, including more equitable funding, incentives for teaching in troubled districts, smaller classes, increased counseling, and options such as apprenticeship programs. Finally, at the college level, they point to programs such as former senator John Edwards's "College for Everyone" in Greene County, North Carolina, which provides one year of public college for students willing to work part-time.

Researchers recommend a variety of measures to help increase the availability of affordable housing, including enforcing antidiscrimination laws to expand housing options for minorities; expanding rent-to-buy programs to help low-income renters become homeowners; and eliminating tax write-offs for high-end real estate.

Strengthening Families

In Akron, Ohio, two billboards displayed the face of a twenty-five-year-old man wanted for nonpayment of $9,594 in child support. A tip from a family member led to the arrest of Giovanni Diaz for criminal nonsupport.

Such measures reflect increased enforcement of child-support orders. Steady child-support payments can make a significant difference in the ability of single-parent families to avoid poverty.

However, once again, researchers say that more can be done. If, for example, child-support payments were automatically deducted from paychecks—and in some cases, they are—collection would be more successful. Policies that effectively hold parents financially responsible for their children might also lead to more cautious early sexual behavior.

But what about young parents who can't or won't pay? If, for example, the noncustodial father has resisted legitimate employment, how can the government collect child support? Programs such as Fathers at Work deal with just such a dilemma. Launched in six sites across the country in 2001, Fathers at Work helped low-income noncustodial fathers (most of whom had committed drug-related offenses) to obtain living-wage jobs and meet their child-support obligations.

Like most of the men in the program, Derrick got into the drug-dealing business for the instant gratification and fast money. Eventually, though, he wearied of the dangers of getting shot or

"Wanted" posters for people who haven't paid their child support are posted on pizza boxes in Hamilton, Ohio.

arrested. Derrick enrolled in Fathers at Work while in a halfway house for criminal offenders. Upon completing the program, he moved in with his girlfriend and found a job working for a friend's business.

"I used to think life was a game and that I could try to get the most money I can, but it didn't work out that way," he told researchers. "So now I'm happy, you know what I mean, just working hard for the money because I'm getting paid good. I got big plans. Pretty soon, hopefully by, I'll say like three months, I'll have me a car."

Boosting Savings and Assets

Aurelio Leonel Alvares-Rosales has a $300-a-week job painting houses in the suburbs of Atlanta, Georgia. Because he didn't earn enough money to set aside the minimum balance required at many banks, he used to cash his payroll check at a twenty-four–hour check-cashing outlet that charged a 3 percent fee. However, thanks to a new financial service outlet in his neighborhood, Alvares-Rosales began to keep more of his hard-earned income.

Some alternative financial institutions have started catering to the estimated nine million households in the United States without bank accounts. Walmart, for instance, operates hundreds of in-store MoneyCenters, which offer such services as check-cashing, money orders, and money transfers.

Savings and assets such as houses provide a much-needed financial cushion to protect against emergencies. However, setting aside money can be particularly difficult for families already feeling the financial pinch. Matching-grant programs, known as Individual Development Accounts, can provide an extra boost. These new programs match private savings with grants from the government, nonprofit organizations, and/or private donors while typically providing financial counseling. Low-interest loans, too, can help. In one case, an immigrant bought a commercial oven to start a home business baking Dominican cakes.

Toward a Brighter Future

Do efforts to fight poverty cost money? Yes, but some of the expenses are ultimately recouped. Investments in education and health care reduce expenditures in prisons and emergency rooms. In such cases, the United States spends resources preventing rather than solving problems.

In public-opinion polls, Americans strongly express their desire for a more equitable society. When asked if they would be willing to pay two hundred dollars a year more in taxes to help the poor, 78 percent of Americans said yes. This would amount to $21 billion to support poverty-reduction initiatives.

In Search of Solutions 121

An alternative to an across-the-board tax increase would be redistributing taxes so that those most in need could see bigger tax cuts or refunds. Over the past thirty years, wealthy households and corporations have benefited dramatically from tax cuts. Closing these loopholes, Rank writes, would result in a more equitable distribution of wealth.

Finally, eliminating poverty might sound impossible, but experts say it's not. Change simply requires a public mandate. As Rank writes, eliminating poverty will come from the simple realization that "impoverishment underprivileges us all."

Tax measures, welfare programs, legislation, job growth, and education all have a role to play in helping people rise above poverty. Finding the right combination remains a challenge, and the needs of the poor may change over time as economic factors shift. The fight against poverty requires an ever-active and -vigilant advocacy for the country's most needy and vulnerable people. Everyone has a role to play in ensuring that the United States remains a land of opportunity.

Glossary

abstinence In this case, the act of refraining from having sex.

contraception The prevention of pregnancy through the use of medication, devices, or techniques; birth control.

crack A type of cocaine that can be smoked; an illegal drug in the United States.

equitable Dealing with or treating fairly all people concerned.

indentured servant A person who has signed a contract binding him or her to work for another person for a specified period of time.

indolence Laziness.

intemperance Lack of moderation, especially when it comes to alcohol and other intoxicants.

internalize To incorporate within the self as conscious or subconscious guiding principles through socialization or learning.

panhandle To stop people and ask them for money or food; to beg.

pauper A very poor person.

poorhouse A place that houses poor and needy people at public expense.

reparations Damages paid to make amends for a wrong or injury.

social safety net A collection of services offered by the state that include welfare programs to protect citizens from poverty.

Social Security A US federal program that provides for the economic security and welfare of citizens, especially when they reach old age.

socioeconomic Relating to a combination of economic and social factors.

stereotype A standardized idea of members of a group that represents a prejudiced attitude or oversimplified opinion.

Further Information

Books

Abramsky, Sasha. *The American Way of Poverty: How the Other Half Still Lives.* New York: National Books, 2013.

Desmond, Matthew. *Evicted: Poverty and Profit in the American City.* New York: Crown Publishing Group, 2016.

Mooney, Linda A., David Knox, and Caroline Schacht. *Understanding Social Problems.* Stamford, CT: Cengage Learning, 2015.

Rios, Dr. Victor. *Punished: Policing the Lives of Black and Latino Boys.* New York: New York University Press, 2011.

Websites

Bureau of Labor Statistics
https://www.bls.gov
This federal agency collects data on the US labor force, including average salaries and reports on the working poor.

Center for American Progress
https://www.americanprogress.org
This nonpartisan policy institute collects research and makes policy recommendations about poverty and other social justice issues.

United States Census Bureau
https://www.census.gov/topics/income-poverty/poverty.html
The US Census Bureau collects comprehensive data on people living in the United States, including information related to income and poverty.

Videos

Surviving the Dust Bowl

http://www.pbs.org/wgbh/americanexperience/films/dustbowl
This PBS documentary tells the story of people who braved hunger and poverty in the Dust Bowl of the central United States during the Great Depression of the 1930s.

What Is Poverty?

https://www.youtube.com/watch?v=U5qig9HIJ7k
This short, animated film explains how physical and social separation contributes to poverty.

What's It Like Living in Poverty?

https://www.youtube.com/watch?v=iVRGpcqNOXg
This short CNN film interviews three women living in poverty as they recount their experiences living in a shelter, dealing with expensive medical problems, and surviving paycheck to paycheck.

Organizations

Canada Without Poverty

251 Bank Street, 5th Floor
Ottawa, Ontario K2P 1X3
(613) 789-0096
http://www.cwp-csp.ca
This nonprofit charity is governed by people who have experienced poverty themselves. It holds that poverty violates human rights and seeks to raise awareness and compile poverty-related research.

Canadian Alliance to End Homelessness

PO Box 15062, Aspen Woods PO
Calgary, AB T3H 0N8
(587) 216-5615
http://caeh.ca

CAEH allies with individuals, communities, and organizations throughout Canada in its mission to end homelessness.

CARE
151 Ellis Street, NE
Atlanta, GA 30303
(800) 422-7385
http://www.care.org
This international organization is committed to ending poverty throughout the globe. It focuses on poverty among women and girls in particular.

Child Poverty Action Group
30 Micawber Street
London, N1 7TB
(202) 657-0640
http://www.childpovertyusa.org
The goal of this organization is to cut child poverty in half over a ten-year period by advocating for policies and strategies aimed at protecting children.

National Coalition for the Homeless
2201 P St. NW
Washington, DC 20037
(202) 462-4822
http://nationalhomeless.org
This nationwide network advocates and provides resources for the homeless with the mission of preventing and ending homelessness.

Oxfam America
226 Causeway Street, 5th Floor
Boston, MA 02114-2206
(800) 776-9326
https://www.oxfamamerica.org
This international organization addresses issues of injustice surrounding poverty. It actively aids people in rising out of poverty and helps people afflicted by natural disasters.

Bibliography

Abelson, Jenn. "Entering the Repossession Lane." *Boston Globe*, March 7, 2008. http://www.boston.com/business/personalfinance/articles/2008/03/07/entering_the_repossession_lane.

"About Teen Pregnancy." Centers for Disease Control and Prevention, May 4, 2017. https://www.cdc.gov/teenpregnancy/about/index.htm.

"Alarming Rate of Drinking and Driving Among Rural Middle Schoolers Found." *Science Daily*, November 2, 2007. http://www.sciencedaily.com/releases/2007/10/071031121528.htm.

Alter, Jonathan. "The Other America: An Enduring Shame." *Newsweek*, September 19, 2005: 42.

Amon, Michael. "As LI Economy Slides, the Newly Poor Seek Assistance." *Chicago Tribune*, Feb. 16, 2008. http://www.chicagotribune.com/topic/ny-lipoo0217,0,5319470.story.

Ash, Jay. Interview by Joan Axelrod-Contrada. March 13, 2008.

Associated Press. "Poverty Shifts to the Suburbs." MSNBC, Dec. 7, 2006. http://www.msnbc.msn.com/id/16077694.

Badger, Emily, Claire Cain Miller, Adam Pearce, and Kevin Quealy. "Extensive Data Shows Punishing Reach of Racism for Black Boys." *New York Times*, March 19, 2018. https://www.nytimes.com/interactive/2018/03/19/upshot/race-class-white-and-black-men.html.

BankForeclosuresSale.com. "A Look at the 2017 Foreclosure Market and the Future in 2018." *Business Insider*, November 20, 2017. http://markets.businessinsider.com/news/stocks/a-look-at-the-2017-foreclosure-market-and-the-future-in-2018-1001549139.

Barello, Stephanie. "Consumer Spending and U.S. Employment from the 2007–2009 Recession through 2022." Monthly Labor Review, US Bureau of Labor Statistics, October 2014. https://www.bls.gov/opub/mlr/2014/article/consumer-spending-and-us-employment-from-the-recession-through-2022.htm.

Barron, David. "American Cities Are Starting to Weigh Up the Pros and Cons of 'Big-Box' Retailers." City Mayors, August 24, 2006. http://www.citymayors.com/economics/bigbox_retailers.html.

Bernstein, Jared. "Economic Mobility in the United States: How Much Is There and Why Does it Matter?" In *Ending Poverty in America: How to Restore the American Dream*, edited by John Edwards, Marion Crain, and Arne L. Kalleberg. Chapel Hill, NC: University of North Carolina at Chapel Hill, 2007.

Berube, Alan, and Elizabeth Kneebone. *Two Steps Back: City and Suburban Poverty Trends 1999–2005*. Washington, DC: Brookings Institution, 2006.

Bosworth, Brandon. "Our Shrinking Underclass." *American Enterprise*, May 2006.

Bradley, James R. "Bridging the Cultures of Business and Poverty: Welfare to Career at Cascade Engineering, Inc." *Stanford Social Innovation Review*, Spring 2003.

"Brief Guide to 2005 TANF Reauthorization Legislation." Center on Budget and Policy Priorities, November 29, 2005, http://www.cbpp.org/4-21-05tanf.pdf.

Broaddus, Matt. "Health Insurance Coverage Reduces Number of People in Poverty." Center on Budget and Policy Priorities, October 20, 2017. https://www.cbpp.org/blog/health-insurance-coverage-reduces-number-of-people-in-poverty.

Brown, David L., and Louis E. Swanson, eds. *Challenges for Rural American in the Twenty-First Century*. University Park, PA: The Pennsylvania State University, 2003.

Brown-Graham, Anita. "Top-Down Meets Bottom-Up: Local Job Creation in Rural America." In *Ending Poverty in America: How to Restore the American Dream*, edited by John Edwards, Marion Crain, and Arne L. Kalleberg. Chapel Hill, NC: University of North Carolina at Chapel Hill, 2007.

Bush, George W. "Let's Get Married." Interview by Alex Kotlowitz. *Frontline*, PBS, November 14, 2002. http://www.pbs.org/wgbh/pages/frontline/shows/marriage/etc/script.html.

"Carlos McBride to Lead New England Public Radio's Media Lab." New England Public Radio, September 22, 2016. https://digital.nepr.net/press-releases/2016/09/22/carlos-mcbride-to-lead-new-england-public-radios-media-lab.

Cauvin, Henri E. "More Families Became Homeless in Recession." *Washington Post*, January 13, 2011. http://www.washingtonpost.com/wp-dyn/content/article/2011/01/12/AR2011011206298.html.

Chappell, Bill. "U.S. Kids Far Less Likely to Out-Earn Their Parents, As Inequality Grows." NPR, December 9, 2016. https://www.npr.org/sections/thetwo-way/2016/12/09/504989751/u-s-kids-far-less-likely-to-out-earn-their-parents-as-inequality-grows.

Chan, Sewell. "Ex-Homeless Man, Loser in Court, Feels Victorious." *New York Times*, May 29, 2006. http://www.nytimes.com/2006/05/29/nyregion/29homeless.html?scp=1&sq=&st=nyt.

"Child Poverty in America." Children's Defense Fund, September 2007. http://www.childrensdefensefund.org.

Chipley, Abigail. "The Hidden Face of Hunger." *Vegetarian Times*, June 2001: 64.

Clampet-Lundquist, Susan. "HOPE VI Relocation: Moving to New Neighborhoods and Building New Ties." *Housing Policy Debate*, Fannie Mae Foundation, 2004. http://www.fanniemaefoundation.org/programs/hpd/pdf/hpd_1502_Clampet.pdf.

Coates, Ta-Nehisi. "The Case for Reparations." *Atlantic*, June 2014. https://www.theatlantic.com/magazine/archive/2014/06/the-case-for-reparations/361631.

Cooper, Eric. "Guarding Against Damaging Implicit Racial Bias — Even In Our Preschools." *HuffPost*, September 27, 2016. https://www.huffingtonpost.com/eric-cooper/guarding-against-damaging_b_12220386.html.

Correspondents of the *New York Times*. *Class Matters*. New York: Times Books, 2003.

Cray, Andrew, Katie Miller, and Laura E. Durso. "Seeking Shelter: The Experiences and Unmet Needs of LGBT Homeless Youth." Center for American Progress, September 2013. https://www.americanprogress.org/wp-content/uploads/2013/09/LGBTHomelessYouth.pdf.

"Criminal Records and Unemployment: The Impact on the Economy." Penn Wharton, University of Pennsylvania: Public Policy Initiative, August 20, 2017. https://publicpolicy.wharton.upenn.edu/live/news/2071-criminal-records-and-unemployment-the-impact-on.

David, Kevin. "Repos in Overdrive: As the Economy Grinds Its Gears, the Vehicle Repossession Rate Is Hitting a Torrid Pace, Keeping Tow Trucks Busy." *Crain's Chicago Business*, July 14, 2003.

Day, Eli. "The Number of Homeless People in America Increased for the First Time in 7 Years." *Mother Jones*, December 21, 2017. https://www.motherjones.com/politics/2017/12/the-number-of-homeless-people-in-america-increased-for-the-first-time-in-7-years.

Derbyshire, Martin. "AGA Numbers Suggest Tribal Gaming Is a $100 Billion Industry." PlayUSA, October 19, 2017. https://www.playusa.com/aga-native-casinos-economic-impact.

Derus, Michele. "Evictions Grow Familiar: As Foreclosures Rise, Days Include Unhappy Surprises for Families." *Milwaukee Journal Sentinel*, June 3, 2007.

Diffey, Louisa, Emily Parker, and Bruce Atchison. "50-State Review." Education Commission of the States, January 2017. https://www.ecs.org/wp-content/uploads/State-Pre-K-Funding-2016-17-Fiscal-Year-Trends-and-opportunities-1.pdf.

Doak, Melissa J. *Social Welfare: Fighting Poverty and Homelessness*. Detroit, MI: Thomson Gale, 2008.

Dolliver, Mark. "Resenting the Rich: How the Rise of Inequality Fosters a New Culture of Antagonism." *Adweek*, December 17, 2007.

Dougherty, Conor. "Tax Overhaul Is a Blow to Affordable Housing Efforts." *New York Times*, January 18, 2018. https://www.nytimes.com/2018/01/18/business/economy/tax-housing.html.

Dreiser, Rodney B. "Jane Addams and the Dream of American Democracy." *Journal of Leisure Research* (Spring 2004): 282.

Dresang, Joel, and Sarah Carr. "Success Depends on an Early Start." *Journal Sentinel* (Milwaukee, WI), March 4, 2006. http://www.jsonline.com.

Duncan, Cynthia M. *Worlds Apart: Why Poverty Persists in Rural America*. New Haven, CT: Yale University Press, 1999.

Eckholm, Erik. "Blue-Collar Jobs Disappear, Taking Families' Way of Life Along." *New York Times*, January 16, 2008.

————. "Program Seeks to Fight Poverty by Building Family Ties." *New York Times*, July 20, 2006. http://query.nytimes.com/gst/fullpage.html?res=9F0CE7DE173FF933A15754C0A9609C8B63.

Edwards, John, Marion Crain, and Arne L. Kalleberg, eds. *Ending Poverty in America: How to Restore the American Dream*. Chapel Hill, NC: University of North Carolina at Chapel Hill, 2007.

Egan, Timothy. "Boredom in the West Fuels Binge Drinking." *New York Times*, September 2, 2006. http://www.nytimes.com/2006/09/02/us/02binge.html.

Fitzgerald, Mike. "Hillbilly Heroin." *Belleville News-Democrat*, September 7, 2003. http://www.opiates.com/media/heroin-belleville.html.

Flanagan, William G., and James Samuelson, "The New Buffalo—But Who Got the Meat?" *Forbes*, September 8, 1997.

Flores, Norma. "On the Border: Migrant Child Labor." *NOW with Bill Moyers*, PBS, May 28, 2004. http://www.pbs.org/now/politics/migrantchildren.html.

Ford, Dana. "Tent City in Suburbs is Cost of Home Crisis." Reuters, December 20, 2007. http://www.reuters.com/article/gc03/idUSN1850682120071221.

Fox, Justin. "Manufacturers Are Hiring, and Hiring." Bloomberg View, March 9, 2018. https://www.bloomberg.com/view/articles/2018-03-09/manufacturing-keeps-adding-jobs-amid-trump-s-tough-talk.

Frey, William H. "Census Shows Nonmetropolitan America Is Whiter, Getting Older, and Losing Population." Brookings Institution, June 27, 2017. https://www.brookings.edu/blog/the-avenue/2017/06/27/census-shows-nonmetropolitan-america-is-whiter-getting-older-and-losing-population.

Futrella, David. "Can Money Buy Happiness?" *Money*, July 8, 2006. http://money.cnn.com/magazines/moneymag/moneymag_archive/2006/08/01/8382225.

Gale, Christopher. "Growing Up Poor." *Teen People*, April 1, 2001.

Girls Incorporated. "Advisory Board Member Profile." *Annual Report*, 2003. http://www.girlsinc.org/ic/content/girlsinc_annualreport_03.pdf.

"Gun Violence in the US Kills More Black People and Urban Dwellers." The Conversation, November 8, 2017. http://theconversation.com/gun-violence-in-the-us-kills-more-black-people-and-urban-dwellers-86825.

Hacker, Jacob S. "The Risky Outlook for Middle-Class America." In *Ending Poverty in America: How to Restore the American Dream*, edited by John Edwards, Marion Crain, and Arne L. Kalleberg. Chapel Hill, NC: University of North Carolina at Chapel Hill, 2007.

Hall, Tex G. "Indian Leader Cites Poverty and Pleads for Aid." *New York Times*, February 1, 2003.

Hamilton, Anita. "Profiting from the Unbanked," *Time*, August 16, 2007. http://www.time.com/time/magazine/article/0,9171,1653666,00.html.

Hankerson, Ashaki. "Let's Get Married." Interview by Alex Kotlowitz. *Frontline*, PBS, November 14, 2002. http://www.pbs.org/wgbh/pages/frontline/shows/marriage/etc/script.html.

Haskins, Ron, Julia B. Isaacs, and Isabel V. Sawhill. *Getting Ahead or Losing Ground: Economic Mobility in America.* Washington, DC: Brookings Institution, 2008.

Hays, Sharon. *Flat Broke with Children: Women in the Age of Welfare Reform*. New York: Oxford University Press, Inc., 2003.

"Homelessness and Housing." Substance Abuse and Mental Health Services Administration, September 15, 2017. https://www.samhsa.gov/homelessness-housing.

House Committee on Education and Labor. "Runaway, Homeless, and Missing Children: Perspectives on Helping the Nation's Vulnerable Youth." Washington: US GPO, 2008.

Hudnut, William H., III. *Halfway to Everywhere: A Portrait of America's First-Tier Suburbs*. Washington, DC: Urban Land Institute, 2004.

"Hunger and Poverty Facts." Feeding America, 2018. http://www.feedingamerica.org/hunger-in-america/hunger-and-poverty-facts.html.

"Hunger Facts: Kids in America Are Hungry." No Kid Hungry, 2018. https://www.nokidhungry.org/who-we-are/hunger-facts.

Iceland, John. *Poverty in America: A Handbook*. Berkeley, CA: University of California Press, 2003.

"In Indian Country." *Economist*, July 10, 1999.

Johnson, Dirk, and Peter Vilbig. "Money Matters: Left Behind Despite the Boom Economy." *New York Times Upfront*, December 13, 1999.

Johnston, David Cay. "Report Says that the Rich are Getting Richer Faster, Much Faster." *New York Times*, December 15, 2007.

"Income Inequality." Inequality.org. Accessed April 13, 2018. https://inequality.org/facts/income-inequality.

"Jane Addams." National-Louis University College of Arts & Sciences. Accessed January 1, 2008. http://www.nl.edu/academics/cas/ace/resources/addams.cfm.

Jillson, Tessa. "Turning toward Acceptance: Cedric Jennings' 'A Hope in the Unseen.'" Gatepost, October 26, 2017. http://fsugatepost.com/2017/10/06/turning-toward-acceptance-cedric-jennings-a-hope-in-the-unseen.

Jones, Charisse. "Crowded Houses Gaining Attention in Suburbs." *USA Today*, January 30, 2006. http://www.usatoday.com/news/nation/2006-01-30-overcrowding-suburbs_x.htm?loc=interstitialskip.

Katz, Michael B. *In the Shadow of the Poorhouse.* New York: Basic Books, Inc., 1986.

Kavilanz, Parija B. "Wal-Mart Expands Low-Cost Banking Services." CNNMoney. com, June 20, 2007. http://money.cnn.com/2007/06020/news/companies/ walmart/index.htm.

Kershaw, Sarah. "Family Behind Foxwoods Loses Hold in Tribe." *New York Times*, June 22, 2007. http://www.nytimes.com/2007/06/22/nyregion/22pequot. html? scp=1&sq=%22Family%20Behind%20Foxwoods%22&st=cse.

Klairmont, Laura. "He Transformed a Trailer into a Free Dental Clinic." CNN, September 22, 2016. https://www.cnn.com/2016/09/22/health/cnn-hero-edwin-smith-kids-first-dental-services/index.html.

Kim, Mingu. "Mental Illness and Homelessness: Facts and Figures." Students in Mental Health Research: A Global Mental Health Initiative, Harvard University, July 31, 2017. http://www.hcs.harvard.edu/~hcht/blog/homelessness-and-mental-health-facts.

Kneebone, Elizabeth. "The Changing Geography of US Poverty." Brookings Institution, February 15, 2017. https://www.brookings.edu/testimonies/the-changing-geography-of-us-poverty.

Kolker, Robert. "A Night on the Streets." *New York*, March 16, 2008.

Kotloff, Lauren J. "Leaving the Street: Young Fathers Move from Hustling to Legitimate Work." Public/Private Ventures, February 2005. http://www.ppv. org/ppv/publications/assets/183_publication.pdf.

Kozol, Jonathan. *The Shame of the Nation: The Restoration of Apartheid Schooling in America.* New York: Crown Publishing Group, 2005.

Krause, Eleanor and Richard V. Reeves. "Rural Dreams: Upward Mobility in America's Countryside." Center on Children and Families, Brookings Institution, September 2017. https://www.brookings.edu/wp-content/ uploads/2017/08/es_20170905_ruralmobility.pdf.

Kristof, Kathy M. "Making Use of Earned Income Tax Credit." *Los Angeles Times*, February 10, 2008. http://articles.latimes.com/2008/feb/10/business/fi-perfin10.

Krogstad, Jens Manuel. "One-in-Four Native Americans and Alaska Natives Are Living in Poverty." Pew Research Center, June 13, 2014. http://www.

pewresearch.org/fact-tank/2014/06/13/1-in-4-native-americans-and-alaska-natives-are-living-in-poverty.

Lapping, Mark B. "Where Problems Persist: One-Sixth of the Nation Is Rural—and Many Rural Residents Are Needy." *Planning*, October 2007.

Laughland, Oliver, and Tom Silverstone. "Liquid Genocide: Alcohol Destroyed Pine Ridge Reservation—Then They Fought Back." *Guardian*, September 29, 2017. https://www.theguardian.com/society/2017/sep/29/pine-ridge-indian-reservation-south-dakota.

Lazaroff, Leon. "One Town's Struggle to Accept Immigrants: An Influx of Immigrants Has Brought Tension—and Violence—to a Long Island Community." *Christian Science Monitor*, July 23, 2003.

Lee-St. John, Jeninne. "A Road Map to Prevention." *Time*, March 26, 2007: 56.

"Lessons Learned: Community-Based Organizations and Career Ladder Training," Bethel New Life, Inc., November 1999. http://www.bethelnewlife.org.

Lindsey, Andrew. "Absolute Poverty vs. Relative Poverty: The Search for Survival." Associated Content. Accessed September 23, 2008. http://www.associatedcontent.com/article/603931/absolute_poverty_vs_relative_poverty.html

Loew, Tracy. "Cities Crack Down on Panhandling." *USA Today*, January 23, 2008.

Long, Heather. "6.3 Million Americans Are 90 Days Late on Their Auto Loan Payments." *Washington Post*, November 14, 2017. https://www.washingtonpost.com/news/wonk/wp/2017/11/14/6-3-million-americans-are-90-days-late-on-their-auto-loan-payments/?utm_term=.70d85cd6dba4.

Lowenstein, Roger. "The Inequality Conundrum." *New York Times Magazine*, June 10, 2007: 11.

"Man Wanted for Nonpayment of Child Support Arrested." *Akron Beacon Journal*, February 8, 2006. http://www.ohio.com/news/break_news/15315041.html.

McBride, Carlos. Interview by Joan Axelrod-Contrada. March 9, 2008.

McDaniels, Abel. "A New Path for School Integration." Center for American Progress, December 19, 2017. https://www.americanprogress.org/issues/education-k-12/news/2017/12/19/444212/new-path-school-integration.

McLanahan, Sarah. "Single Mothers, Fragile Families." In *Ending Poverty in America: How to Restore the American Dream*, edited by John Edwards, Marion Crain, and Arne L. Kalleberg. Chapel Hill, NC: University of North Carolina at Chapel Hill, 2007.

———, and Gary Sandefur. *Growing Up with a Single Parent: What Hurts, What Helps* Cambridge, MA: Harvard University Press, 1994.

Meltzer, Milton. *Poverty in America*. New York: William Morrow & Co., Inc., 1986.

"The Mendacity Index." *Washington Monthly*, September 2003. http://www.washingtonmonthly.com/features/2003/030,mendacity-index.html.

Mendez Cassell, Carol. "A Hopeful Future: The Path to Helping Teens Avoid Pregnancy and Too-Soon Parenthood." In *Ending Poverty in America: How to Restore the American Dream*, edited by John Edwards, Marion Crain, and Arne L. Kalleberg. Chapel Hill, NC: University of North Carolina at Chapel Hill, 2007.

"Mental Illness." National Institute of Mental Health, November 2017. https://www.nimh.nih.gov/health/statistics/mental-illness.shtml.

Mintz, S. "The Origins of New World Slavery." University of Houston. Accessed January 2, 2008. http://www.digitalhistory.uh.edu.

Murray, Charles. *Losing Ground: American Social Policy 1950–1980*. New York: Basic Books, Inc., 1984.

Muskie School of Public Service. "Substance Abuse Among Rural Youth: A Little Meth and a Lot of Booze." Research & Policy Brief, June 2007. http://muskie.usm.maine.edu/Publications/rural/pb35.pdf.

Nanez, Dianna M. "'Don't Ask, Don't Tell' Immigration Era Ending." *Arizona Republic*, April 24, 2007. http://www.azcentral.com/arizonarepublic/local articles/0424deportation0424.html.

Newman, Katherine S., and Victor Tan Chen. *The Missing Class: Portraits of the Near Poor in America*. Boston, MA: Beacon Books, 2007.

"The 1996 Personal Responsibility and Work Opportunity Reconciliation Act in the US." Centre for Public Impact, October 30, 2017. https://www.centreforpublicimpact.org/case-study/personal-responsibility-and-work-opportunity-reconciliation-act-the-clinton-welfare-reform.

"Obama's Focus Is Responsibility in NAACP Speech." CNN, July 14, 2008. http://www.cnn.com/2008/POLITICS/07/14/obama.naacp/index.html.

Olasky, Marvin. *The Tragedy of American Compassion*. Washington, DC: Regnery Gateway, 1992.

Partelow, Lisette, Angie Spong, Catherine Brown, and Stephenie Johnson. "America Needs More Teachers of Color and a More Selective Teaching Profession." Center for American Progress, September 14, 2017. https://www.americanprogress.org/issues/education-k-12/reports/2017/09/14/437667/america-needs-teachers-color-selective-teaching-profession.

Payne, Ruby K. *A Framework for Understanding Poverty*. Highlands, TX: aha! Process, Inc., 2005.

Philips, Matthew. "OK, Sister, Drop That Sandwich! Cities Fight Panhandling by Outlawing Food Giveaways in Parks." *Newsweek*, November 6, 2006.

"Pine Ridge Indian Reservation." Re-member.org, 2018. https://www.re-member.org/pine-ridge-reservation.aspx.

"Poverty Thresholds." United States Census Bureau, January 19, 2018. https://www.census.gov/data/tables/time-series/demo/income-poverty/historical-poverty-thresholds.html.

Press, Eyal. "The New Suburban Poverty." *Nation*, April 23, 2007. http://www.thenation.com/doc/20070423/press.

"Primary Source Document: Lyndon B. Johnson: The War on Poverty." *Encyclopaedia Britannica Online*. Accessed January 4, 2008. http://www.britannica.com/eb/article-9116920.

"Psychologist Produces the First-ever 'World Map of Happiness.'" *ScienceDaily*, November 14, 2006. http://www.sciencedaily.com/releases/2006/11/061113093726.htm.

Quezada, Angelina. "Separate Is Still Unequal." Center for American Progress, February 22, 2018. https://www.americanprogress.org/issues/education-k-12/news/2018/02/22/447098/separate-still-unequal.

Qullian, Lincoln, and Rozlyn Redd. "Can Social Capital Explain Persistent Racial Poverty Gaps?" National Poverty Center Working Paper Series, June 2006. http://www.npc.umich.edu/publications/workingpaper06/paper12/working_paper06-12.pdf.

Rank, Mark Robert. *One Nation, Underprivileged: Why American Poverty Affects Us All*. New York: Oxford University Press, 2004.

Roach, Rebecca. "It Happens to 'Good Girls' Too." About.com: Teen Advice. Accessed January 16, 2008. http://teenadvice.about.com/library/weekly/aa122100a.htm.

Rothwell, Jonathan. "How the War on Drugs Damages Black Social Mobility." Brookings, September 30, 2014. https://www.brookings.edu/blog/social-mobility-memos/2014/09/30/how-the-war-on-drugs-damages-black-social-mobility.

Schwartz, Stephanie M. "The Arrogance of Ignorance: Hidden Away, Out of Sight and Out of Mind." *Native Village Youth and Education News*, October 15, 2006. http://www.nativevillage.org/Messages%20from%20the%20People/the%20arrogance%20of%20ignorance.htm.

Scott, Michael S. "Panhandling." Center for Problem Oriented Policing, Guide No. 13, 2002. http://www.popcenter.org/problems/panhandling.

Semega, Jessica L., Kayla R. Fontenot, and Melissa A. Kollar. "Income and Poverty in the United States: 2016." United States Census Bureau, September 12, 2017. https://www.census.gov/library/publications/2017/demo/p60-259.html.

Shipler, David K. *The Working Poor: Invisible in America*. New York: Alfred A. Knopf, 2004.

Shulman, Beth. *The Betrayal of Work: How Low-Wage Jobs Fail 30 Million Americans*. New York: The New Press, 2003.

———. "Making Work Pay." In *Ending Poverty in America: How to Restore the American Dream*, edited by John Edwards, Marion Crain, and Arne L. Kalleberg. Chapel Hill, NC: University of North Carolina at Chapel Hill, 2007.

Sinclair, Elizabeth. "Research Weekly: Homelessness Increases Among Individuals with Serious Mental Illness." Treatment Advocacy Center, January 11, 2018. http://www.treatmentadvocacycenter.org/fixing-the-system/features-and-news/3965-research-weekly-homelessness-increases-among-individuals-with-serious-mental-illness-.

Sitrin, Carly. "Teen Birth Rates Just Hit an All-Time Low." Vox, June 30, 2017. https://www.vox.com/science-and-health/2017/6/30/15894750/teen-birth-rates-hit-all-time-low.

Smith Hopkins, Jamie. "Families Discuss 'Living Wage.'" *Baltimore Sun*, May 6, 2007. http://progressivemaryland.org/files/public/documents/CLIPS-PM-intheNews/2007May-Dec/2007-5-06-bsun-hucker-familiesdiscusslivingwage.pdf.

Stanford Center on Poverty and Inequality. "State of the Union: The Poverty and Inequality Report." Pathways, 2016. https://inequality.stanford.edu/sites/default/files/Pathways-SOTU-2016.pdf.

"A State of Hunger: Improving Washington's Food Stamp Program." Washington Citizen Action, June 2002, http://nwfco.org/06-01-02_WCA_A_State_of_Hunger.pdf.

"Statement of Alan Berube, Fellow, The Brookings Institution." Subcommittee on Income Security and Family Support of the House Committee on Ways and Means, 110th Congress, February 13, 2007. http://waysandmeans.house.gov/hearings.asp?formmode=view&id=5452.

"Steady on the Tequila: Drunk Driving in New Mexico." *Economist*, March 17, 2007.

Stein, Joel. "The Real Faces of Homelessness." *Time*, January 20, 2003.

"Study: White and Black Children Biased Toward Lighter Skin." CNN, May 14, 2010. http://www.cnn.com/2010/US/05/13/doll.study/index.html.

Subcommittee on Human Resources. "A Decade Since Welfare Reform: 1996 Welfare Reforms Reduce Welfare Dependence." House Committee on Ways and Means, February 26, 2006. http://waysandmeans.house.gov/media/pdf/welfare/022706welfare.pdf.

"Success Stories." Culinary Training Academy, Las Vegas, NV. Accessed May 30, 2008. http://www.theculinaryacademy.org.

"Success Stories—Welfare to Work Vouchers." US Department of Housing and Urban Development. Accessed June 17, 2008. http://www.hud.gov/offices/pih/programs/hcv/wtw/ppp/success.cfm.

Summers, Juana. "Looming Trump Budget Cuts Deepen Distress on Pine Ridge." CNN, May 28, 2017. https://www.cnn.com/2017/05/27/politics/indian-reservation-trump-budget/index.html.

"Survey Links Racial Views to Obama's Polls Numbers." Fox News, September 20, 2008. http://elections.foxnews.com/2008/09/20/survey-links-racial-views-to-obamas-polls-numbers.

"Surviving the Dust Bowl." *The American Experience*, PBS, March 2, 1998. http://www.pbs.org/wgbh/americanexperience/films/dustbowl.

Suskind, Ron. *A Hope in the Unseen: An American Odyssey from the Inner City to the Ivy League*. New York: Broadway Books, 2005.

Taylor, Keeanga-Yamahtta. "Barack Obama's Original Sin: America's Post-Racial Illusion." *Guardian*, January 13, 2017. https://www.theguardian.com/us-news/2017/jan/13/barack-obama-legacy-racism-criminal-justice-system.

"Teen Pregnancy Prevention." National Conference of State Legislatures, March 12, 2018. http://www.ncsl.org/research/health/teen-pregnancy-prevention.aspx.

Thiede, Brian, Lillie Greiman, Stephan Weiler, Steven Beda, and Tessa Conroy. "6 Charts That Illustrate the Divide between Rural and Urban America." PBS, March 17, 2017. https://www.pbs.org/newshour/nation/six-charts-illustrate-divide-rural-urban-america.

Torrey, E. Fuller, and Mary Zdanowicz. "Why Deinstitutionalization Turned Deadly." *Wall Street Journal*, August 4, 1998. http://www.psychlaws.orgGeralResources/Article2.htm.

"2015 FDIC National Survey of Unbanked and Underbanked Households." Federal Deposit Insurance Corporation, June 29, 2017. https://www.fdic.gov/householdsurvey.

"The 2017 Annual Homeless Assessment Report (AHAR) to Congress." US Department of Housing and Urban Development, Office of Community Planning and Development, December 2017. https://www.hudexchange.info/resources/documents/2017-AHAR-Part-1.pdf.

Tyre, Peg, and Matthew Phillips. "Poor Among Plenty: For the First Time, Poverty Shifts to the US Suburbs." *Newsweek*, February 12, 2007.

Urbina, Ian. "In Kentucky's Teeth: Toll of Poverty and Neglect." *New York Times*, December 24, 2007.

"Veterans and Military Families." Substance Abuse and Mental Health Services Administration, September 15, 2017. https://www.samhsa.gov/veterans-military-families.

Warren, Elizabeth. "The Vanishing Middle Class." In *Ending Poverty in America: How to Restore the American Dream*, edited by John Edwards, Marion Crain, and Arne L. Kalleberg. Chapel Hill, NC: University of North Carolina at Chapel Hill, 2007.

Washington Post Staff. "What Trump Proposed Cutting in His 2019 Budget." *Washington Post*, February 16, 2018. https://www.washingtonpost.com/graphics/2018/politics/trump-budget-2019/?utm_term=.d04223f5b37b.

Weese, Karen. "Why It Costs So Much to Be Poor in America." *Washington Post*, January 25, 2018. https://www.washingtonpost.com/news/posteverything/wp/2018/01/25/why-it-costs-so-much-to-be-poor-in-america/?utm_term=.af0e92449dbe.

Weir, Bill, and Sylvia Johnson. "Denmark: The Happiest Place on Earth." ABC News, January 8, 2007. http://abcnews.go.com/2020/story?id=4086092&page=1.

Westfall, Sandra Sobieraj, and Bill Hewitt. "Barack Obama Makes History!" *People*, November 17, 2008.

White, Gillian B. "The Black and Hispanic Unemployment Rates Don't Deserve Applause." *Atlantic*, January 8, 2018. https://www.theatlantic.com/business/archive/2018/01/trump-black-hispanic-unemployment/549932.

Wilson, William Julius. "When Work Disappears: New Implications for Race and Urban Poverty in the Global Economy." London School of Economics, November 1998. http://ideas.repec.org/p/cep/sticas/17.html.

W. K. Kellogg Foundation. "Chelsea, Massachusetts." Kellogg Leadership for Community Change. Accessed March 13, 2008. http://kkf.org/Default.aspx?tabid=90&CID=276&ItemID=2760047&NID=2770047&LanguageID=0.

Wolf, Richard. "How Welfare Reform Changed America." *USA Today*, July 18, 2006. http://www.usatoday.com/news/nation/2006-07-17-welfare-reform-cover_x.htm.

Index

Page numbers in **boldface** are illustrations.

abstinence, 44
Addams, Jane, 14–15, **15**
African American, 7–8, 13, 16, 19, 21, 26, 30–31, 33, 45, 66–71, 75, 77–78, 84, 93, 99

Bush, President George W., 50, 88–89, 108

Centers for Disease Control and Prevention (CDC), 42–43, 71
childcare, 7–9, 36, 42, 50, 62, 104–105, 109, 118–119
civil rights, 8, 18, 69, 102
class, 25–28, 30, 32, 36, 47, 49, 57, 59–60, 63, 74, 92–93, 106, 114, 116
Coates, Ta-Nehisi, **28–29**, 31
contraception, 44
crack, 36, 100, 103–104

day laborers, 6, 57–58
debt, 7, 23, 26, 111
deportation, 34, 88
disposable income, 26, 62
drug abuse, 55, **91**, 98

economic mobility, 8, 93
equitable, 118, 121–122

Fathers at Work, 119–120
food insecurity, 39–42
food stamps, 18, 39, 85

globalization, 9
Great Depression, 17, 70, 114
Great Recession, 33, 53–54, 60–61, 65, 111, 117
Great Society, 19

Hispanic, 7, 26, 66–67, 70, 77, 99
homelessness, **4**, 6, 17, 38, 48, **64**, **94**, 95–103, **101**, **103**, 111, **112**, 113, 117
Hoover, Herbert, 17

immigrants, 12, 16, 32, 34–35, 54–59, **59**, 89, 121
Immigration and Customs Enforcement (ICE), 34
incarceration rates, 30, 43, 50, 69
indentured servant, **10**, 12
indolence, 13
intemperance, 13
intergenerational mobility, 8, 81
internalize, 68
internment camps, 32

Jennings, Cedric, 75, **76**, 78–79

Johnson, President Lyndon B., 18

Kennedy, Robert F., 19, **20–21**

living wage, 9, 110, 119

Medicaid, 18, 116

Medicare, 18

mental illness, 97

migrant workers, 84, **87**, 88

minimum wage, 36, 108–110

minorities, 7, 9, 31, 71, 75, 77–78, 96, 99, 119

National Association for the Advancement of Colored People (NAACP), 68–69

Native Americans, 7, 26, 84–85, **85**, 99

New Deal, 17, 114

Obama, President Barack, 23, 34–35, 50, 66–69, **70**

outsourcing, 32, 108

panhandle, 100

Patient Protection and Affordable Care Act, 23, 44, 116–117

pauper, 13

Personal Responsibility and Work Opportunity Reconciliation Act (PRWORA), 22, 104

poorhouse, 8, 13, 16, 113

poverty line, 5, 26, 39–40, 51, 53–54, 74, 85

racism, 21, 30–31, 58, 65–67

Rank, Mark, 9, 114, 122

reparations, 30–32

Roosevelt, President Franklin D., 17, 114

rural areas, 9, 65, 81–84, 89–91

segregation, 8, 77

settlement houses, 14

single parenting, 7, 41–42, 45–46, 77, 114, 117, 119

slavery, 8, 12–13, 16, 31, 66, 93

social safety net, 114

Social Security, 18, 89, 114

Social Security Act, 17

socioeconomic, 21, 33, 78, 81

stereotype, 21, 66–68, 72, 83

suburbs, 8, 18, 22, 53–59, 65, 82, 100, 117, 120

Temporary Assistance for Needy Families program, 22–23, 104

unemployment, 45, 50, 70–71, 95, 111, 113

unions, 9, 19, 66, 108–109, **109**

urban areas, 9, 18, 22, 40, 45, 54–55, 65–66, 71, 74–75, 77, 79, 81–83, 90

US Department of Housing and
Urban Development (HUD),
98–99, 117

veterans, 98–99

welfare programs, 13, 17, **24**, **49**,
122
welfare reform, 8, 22, 48, 69,
104–105, 113
welfare-to-work programs, 22,
104–106, **107**, 116
Works Progress Administration
(WPA), 17
World War II, 17, 32

About the Authors

Joan Axelrod-Contrada is the author of fifteen books for middle-school and high-school students. She has written about a variety of topics, including women leaders, the Lizzie Borden trial, and colonial America. Her work has also appeared in the *Boston Globe* and various other publications. She lives in western Massachusetts.

Erin L. McCoy is a literature, language, and cultural studies educator and an award-winning photojournalist and poet. She holds a master of arts degree in Hispanic studies and a master of fine arts degree in creative writing from the University of Washington. She has edited nearly twenty nonfiction books for young adults, including *The Mexican-American War and The Israel-Palestine Border Conflict* from the Redrawing the Map series with Cavendish Square Publishing. She is from Louisville, Kentucky.